ASPIRING TO FREEDOM

ASPIRING TO FREEDOM

Commentaries on John Paul II's Encyclical
The Social Concerns of the Church

by

Peter L. Berger, Richard John Neuhaus,
Michael Novak, Roberto Suro, and George Weigel

Edited by

Kenneth A. Myers

with

the Complete Text of the Encyclical

WILLIAM B. EERDMANS PUBLISHING COMPANY
GRAND RAPIDS, MICHIGAN

The essays by Peter L. Berger, Richard John Neuhaus, Michael Novak,
and George Weigel were first published in *This World*.
Roberto Suro's essay was first published in *Crisis*.

Library of Congress Cataloging-in-Publication Data

Aspiring to freedom.

1. Catholic Church. Pope (1978-   : John Paul II).
Sollicitudo rei socialis.   2. Sociology, Christian
(Catholic) —Papal documents.   I. Berger, Peter L.
II. Myers, Kenneth A.
BX1753.C34   1987 Suppl.   261.8   88-16563

ISBN 0-8028-0412-8

Contents

Introduction

RICHARD JOHN NEUHAUS

The encyclical that is the occasion for this book has already sparked a vigorous discussion. There is lively disagreement about what in fact the pope is saying, and about the merits of what he is saying. It is not surprising that people with definite viewpoints on the questions addressed by this encyclical are tempted to cite the document somewhat selectively. The authors of the essays in this book are not immune to that temptation. Whether the text be an encyclical or the United States Constitution or the Bible, we all have a tendency to invoke passages that support our prejudices and to downplay or ignore those passages that are inconvenient to the argument we would make. I hope the reader will recognize that temptation in interpreting *Sollicitudo Rei Socialis*. It will become apparent, I believe, that in these essays most particular attention is paid to passages and concerns that seem to be in tension with what the several writers believe the encyclical intends to say, or should intend to say.

We do not assume that every reader of this book is a student of Roman Catholic social teaching. On the contrary, we expect that many readers are not Roman Catholic at all, and until now may have had only a marginal interest in papal social thought. For such readers, but not for them alone, a word may be in order about the nature of encyclicals and the guidelines for interpreting them.

An encyclical is, quite simply, a circular letter. The Apostle Paul's letters in the New Testament might be called encyclicals, since they were circulated among the churches. It is a form of

communication frequently used by popes, especially since
Benedict XIV in the eighteenth century. An encyclical carries
more weight of authority than a pastoral letter or apostolic exhortation, but not as much weight as, say, an apostolic constitution. Encyclicals are intended to be taken very seriously by
anyone who takes the pope seriously, and I suggest that we all
have reason to take this pope very seriously indeed. It used to
be that encyclicals were addressed to the bishops and, often, to
the Roman Catholic faithful. John XXIII began, and his succes-
sors have continued, the practice of addressing them also to "all
people of good will." The present encyclical, *Sollicitudo Rei Socialis* ("The Social Concerns of the Church") most particularly
addresses Christians who are not Roman Catholic, as well as
Jews, Muslims, and people of other religions.

An encyclical is by no means an "infallible" pronouncement.
The last pope who officially spoke in the infallible mode was Pius
XII when in 1950 he promulgated the dogma of the bodily as-
sumption of the Virgin Mary. To say that an encyclical is not infallible, however, does not mean that it is nothing more than the
pope's opinion. Orthodox Roman Catholics believe that the ministry of the papacy is attended by "the special assistance of the
Holy Spirit." There is, therefore, a strong presumption of agreement with and obedience to papal pronouncements on matters
of faith and morals. That is somewhat more than simply saying
that, on matters of faith and morals, the pope should be given the
benefit of the doubt. In 1950, Pius XII said, "In writing such letters the popes do not exercise the supreme power of their teaching authority." That language was adopted by Vatican Council II
in the "Constitution on the Church." The Council pointedly did
not adopt Pius's additional statement that, when an encyclical
takes a stand on a controverted subject, it "can no longer be re-
garded as a matter for free debate among theologians."

The practical authority of encyclicals was weakened by the
reaction to *Humanae Vitae,* which dealt with human reproduc-
tion and was issued by Paul VI in 1968. Liberal Catholicism,
which almost certainly includes most of the theological establishment, vigorously and publicly protested that encyclical's
teaching, especially on contraception. According to some students of Catholicism in America, the reaction to *Humanae Vitae*
did more than any other one thing to undermine confidence in

the teaching authority of the pope. *The Encyclopedic Dictionary of Religion*, published under Roman Catholic auspices, blithely states, "The consensus today is that no generalization may be made about the teaching authority of encyclicals. Each must be judged on its individual merits." One may reasonably assume that Pope John Paul II was not consulted in the establishment of that consensus.

The fact remains, however, that even those Catholics who incline to the view that an encyclical is nothing more than the pope's opinion do quote papal pronouncements—sometimes very selectively—to show that the pope is "on our side." It must be admitted also that some "traditionalist" Catholics who attribute near-infallibility to every papal utterance are, when faced by a disagreeable encyclical, skilled at explaining why the pope did not say what for all the world he appears to have said. Probably most Roman Catholics who read encyclicals at all try to accord them the respect due the chief teaching office in the church. An encyclical is not the final word. It is not necessarily even the most felicitous word. But, in both theory and practical influence, it also is not merely one opinion among others.

Those of us who are not Roman Catholic also have good reason to read this encyclical with care. Of course Protestant and Eastern Orthodox Christians do not accept all, or even most, of the claims for papal authority. Many Protestants, notably Lutherans and Anglicans, are prepared to recognize that the pope might exercise a "petrine ministry" and "teaching primacy" in a reunited Church. Many other Protestants, notably fundamentalists, are decidedly less well disposed to the papacy. They make no bones of the fact that they believe the pope is the Antichrist, the "man of sin" referred to in 2 Thessalonians 2. So on this, as on many other questions, the differences among Protestant Christians are much greater than the differences between some Protestants and Roman Catholics. Despite these differences, however, everyone who wants to understand the historical situation of Christianity at the edge of the twenty-first century has reason to pay attention to what is said by the pope, and by this pope in particular. In terms of practical influence, John Paul II is the premier Christian teacher of our time. Whether or not we agree with what he says, whether or not we accept the claims made for his office, more Christians are more influenced over a longer period of time by the words of the pope than by those of any other Christian leader. Thus indifference to the ministry of the pope is indifference to the course of Christianity in the contemporary world.

For Roman Catholics, and certainly for other Christians, not everything the pope says is of equal weight. Nor is something true just because the pope says it. In Roman Catholic teaching, the pope's particular authority *as pope* is on questions of "faith and morals." In addition, Roman Catholic teaching is clear that the pope is in no way an independent agent. From the Council of Trent, following the sixteenth-century division of the Church in the West, through Vatican Council I which defined papal infallibility, through Vatican Council II only a quarter of a century ago, Roman Catholic teaching is clear that the pope is the servant of Christ and the Church. He must act always in communion with his fellow bishops and in obedience to Scripture and the received tradition. The pope cannot "invent" a new doctrine, as that development is sustained by the *sensus fidelium* (the sense of the faithful who are the Church). This does not mean that church teaching is put to a vote and determined by a majority of Catholics, or by a majority of theologians. In this sense, the Roman Catholic Church is decidedly undemocratic. But then, so is any other community of Christians who seriously believe that Christ is prophet, priest, and king.

In reading an encyclical, criteria of judgment must be employed, discriminations must be made. The pope's words are more authoritative when he explicitly connects what he is saying to the scriptural tradition that he is pledged to serve. They are less authoritative when he is simply expressing his views about a matter of fact in the contemporary world. We may think he is right or wrong in either case, but these different kinds of statement carry different weight. In the present encyclical, for example, what John Paul says about the human "aspiration to freedom" is clearly and explicitly grounded in a Christian theology of creation and human nature. What he says about the comparable "imperialism" of East and West is just as clearly grounded in his personal understanding of the geopolitics of the contemporary world. For the reasons mentioned above, both assertions should be given serious consideration. But, formally and substantively, they are assertions of very different orders of authority. It is an oddity of our day that many Catholics who express the greatest doubt about papal authority are most inclined to embrace those papal statements that are least authoritative. That oddity has been pronounced in the published comment on *Sollicitudo* to date.

No doubt some will question the way in which the commentaries in this book emphasize some aspects of the encyclical over others. That is to be expected and is part of what will certainly be the continuing discussion of this important document. Probably the most significant disputes are hermeneutical, that is, disputes over the rules for interpreting a document such as this. A critically important rule, whether in interpreting Scripture, a Supreme Court decision, or a papal encyclical, is to attend to the context. The context for Roman Catholic social teaching goes back to *Rerum Novarum*, issued by Leo XIII in 1891. More immediately, the context for understanding this encyclical includes the many other statements by John Paul II, and especially his other encyclicals. In the first year of his pontificate, 1979, he issued *Redemptor Hominis* ("The Redeemer of Man"), which, among other things, sought to advance the understanding of a Christian anthropology. *Dives in Misericordia* ("Rich in Mercy") was a 1980 encyclical underscoring the limits of purely secular understandings of justice. Nineteen eighty-one saw *Laborem Exercens* ("On Human Work"), which is closely related to what the pope says in the present encyclical about man as the "protagonist" in historical change. *Slavorum Apostoli* ("Apostles to the Slavs") in 1985 highlighted the spiritual and cultural unity of East and West in the history of Europe. In 1986, *Dominum et Vivificantem* ("The Holy Spirit in the Church and World") offered a devotional-theological understanding of the work of the Spirit in creation and in the personal and communal life of Christians. All are important, of course, to understanding the mind of John Paul, but the first three are especially pertinent to the interpretation of *Sollicitudo*, this pope's most recent encyclical.

Most of the comment about the present encyclical has focused on John Paul's criticisms of the "superdeveloped" countries of the West. We in the West are sharply divided in our response to such criticism. On the one hand, many of our intellectuals are much given to self-criticism, even to self-flagellation. With respect to Western culture in general and American society in particular, the worst that can be said does not say the half of it. On the other hand, Americans less susceptible to masochism may feel offended by some of the harsh things the pope says with (apparently) our society in mind. We do well to guard against excessive defensiveness. After all, there are harsh things that need saying about our society. In truth, those who admire this pope and those who have little use for him are both likely to welcome his harsh words, but they will welcome different harsh words. One party cheers his condemnation of a society that tolerates the killing of the unborn, celebrates cultural decadence, and succumbs to moral relativism in personal and family life. The other party applauds John Paul's criticism of a "liberal capitalism" that exploits workers, creates unemployment, and oppresses the poor of the world. It is not that one party cares more about "the moral issues" than the other. It is that they define "the moral issues" differently or, if they agree on the issues, they arrange them in different hierarchies. We have, in short, moral agendas in conflict. *Sollicitudo* cannot resolve that conflict, and should not be used selectively to enlist support for one agenda or the other. It can be read critically and appreciatively as a contribution to a debate that is almost certain to occupy us for years to come.

Many American Catholics are given to saying, "the pope does not understand us." As often as not, that means, "the pope does not agree with us." But behind such complaints there is also a widespread suspicion that this pope does not really like America very much, and that he likes many of the leaders and movers in American Catholicism even less. I doubt that the first part of that suspicion is accurate, but it raises a question which Michael Novak touches on briefly in his commentary in this volume. The question is whether John Paul, looking ahead to the Church and the world of the third millennium, is giving up on the West and, more specifically, on the United States. Of course one hopes that is not the case. But it has been said of the Vatican, "you can always count on Rome to come to terms with the barbarians." That may be unfair both to Rome and to those who are called barbarians, but there is a rough wisdom in the saying. As leader of the most universal of churches, the pope has no choice but to take a long-term view of world-historical change, of the waxings and the wanings of peoples and powers.

The centers of spiritual vibrancy and growth seem to be shifting to the "Third World" of which the present encyclical is so solicitous. Surely John Paul has not been unaffected by the dramatic contrast between, for example, his reception in Holland and his reception when visiting the continent of Africa. In Holland a besieged church tries to keep alive a semblance of Catholic identity and to provide for the pope a narrowed space of hospitality in an alienated culture dominated by the host of decadences which John Paul associates with *"superdevelopment."* Reflecting on Europe more generally, the pope has repeatedly spoken in elegiac tones about the decline of the West—the decline of faith, the decline of cultural confidence, even the decline of population.

As for the United States, as rich and influential as American Catholicism may be, it constitutes only seven percent of the church's membership. That so few should dominate so much— in economics, in communications, in church politics—is deeply resented by many others. Echoes of that resentment are to be heard in *Sollicitudo*. Moreover, the Vatican has long been alert to openings to the East. An explicit "Oest Politik" was pursued by Paul VI. Vatican observers note that, while that policy has not been repudiated by John Paul, it certainly has taken some different turns. This pope—with his powerful ties to Poland and the churches of Central and Eastern Europe—is by no means resigned, as many people thought Paul VI was resigned, to the political status quo of the Soviet bloc. As prepared as he is to challenge that status quo, however, it is possible that he has only modest expectations with respect to the success of that challenge. Between the "two blocs" pondered in this encyclical, the pope, looking twenty and fifty years ahead, may be reckoning on the ascendancy of the East. Maybe the best the church can do is to embrace the ideas of political freedom and human rights nurtured in the West, and hope that that will have some influence in tempering the rule of the barbarians when they take over. In this view of things, the West has lost its will to survive, never mind its determination to be the history-forming force of the future.

I do not say that this is John Paul's view of the world. But there are intimations of such a view in *Sollicitudo*. If this is the view that prevails in the Vatican, Rome must ask itself whether it is not reinforcing the drift that it deplores. If the Western democracies are as culturally decadent, as spiritually exhausted, and as baneful in their effect on the rest of the world as *Sollicitudo* may be suggesting, then certainly there is good reason for the West to be suffering a loss of will. If even the military preparedness of the West is the product of excessive fears about security, as *Sollicitudo* does suggest, then the appropriate course might be disarmament militarily as well as culturally. One must wonder whether this pope understands that some of what he seems to be saying is interpreted in the West not as a call to conversion but as a counsel to resignation.

In addition, and despite John Paul's personalist opposition to determinisms of all sorts, there seems to be an element of economic determinism in his reflections on the "structures of sin" to which we are, or so it would appear, captive. Finally, in this and many of his other statements, the pope seems not to differentiate sufficiently between Europe and the United States. There is some reason for speaking of Western European countries as "post-Christian." Spiritually, culturally, economically, and demographically, some of those societies are manifestly in decline. In America, however, there are those who hope for a "Catholic Moment"—a historical moment in which the Roman Catholic Church assumes a role of leadership in restoring moral legitimacy to the institutions of a society fit for free persons. It would be most unfortunate were *Sollicitudo* to be interpreted in a manner that undermines this sense of possibility, and of responsibility. In failing to appreciate the distinctiveness of what John Courtney Murray called "the American proposition," the Vatican could be contributing powerfully, albeit inadvertently, to the "Europeanization" of America. I am certain that is not the intention of this pope, but in tone, if not in substance, he may at times be working against his best intentions.

The writers of the four essays in this volume had different assignments. Michael Novak was asked to analyze *Sollicitudo* with an eye to what it says about the development of Catholic social teaching on economics and political economy. Peter Berger was asked to examine the encyclical in the light of what we know about the empirical evidence for what does, and what does not, make for development. George Weigel's analysis addresses the questions of the institutions of liberal democracy, with special reference to Murray's "American proposition." My assignment was to examine the moral and theo-logic of *Sollicitudo*. Finally, Roberto Suro, chief of the Rome bureau of the *New York Times*, offers the result of his investigations into the procedure that produced the encyclical. Quite unsurprisingly, at points each of the writers invades the turf of the others. I view that overlapping as a definite strength of this discussion, since it demonstrates how some aspects of the encyclical can reasonably be interpreted in quite different ways.

Four of these essays originally appeared as a symposium in *This World: A Journal of Religion and Public Life*, the quarterly published by The Rockford Institute Center on Religion and Society. Roberto Suro's analysis was first published in *Crisis*. We are indebted to Kenneth Myers, editor of *This World*, for his skillful shepherding of this project through to its present form, and to Katherine Maly, who provided invaluable editorial assistance.

Encyclical Letter

SOLLICITUDO REI SOCIALIS

of the Supreme Pontiff

John Paul II

to the Bishops
Priests
Religious Families
Sons and Daughters
of the Church
and All People of Good Will
for the
Twentieth Anniversary of
Populorum Progressio

On Social Concern

Venerable Brothers
and dear Sons and Daughters,
Health and the Apostolic Blessing!

I. Introduction

1. The social concern of the Church, directed towards an authentic development of man and society which would respect and promote all the dimensions of the human person, has always expressed itself in the most varied ways. In recent years, one of the special means of intervention has been the Magisterium of the Roman Pontiffs which, beginning with the Encyclical *Rerum Novarum* of Leo XIII as a point of reference,[1] has frequently dealt with the question and has sometimes made the dates of publication of the various social documents coincide with the anniversaries of that first document.[2]

The Popes have not failed to throw fresh light by means of those messages upon new aspects of the social doctrine of the Church. As a result, this doctrine, beginning with the outstanding contribution of Leo XIII and enriched by the successive contributions of the Magisterium, has now become an updated doctrinal "corpus." It builds up gradually, as the Church, in the

---

1. Leo XIII, Encyclical *Rerum Novarum* (May 15, 1891): *Leonis XIII P. M. Acta*, XI, Romae 1892, pp. 97-144.

2. Pius XI, Encyclical *Quadragesimo Anno* (May 15, 1931): *AAS* 23 (1931), pp. 177-228; John XXIII, Encyclical *Mater et Magistra* (May 15, 1961): *AAS* 53 (1961), pp. 401-464; Paul VI, Apostolic Letter *Octogesima Adveniens* (May 14, 1971): *AAS* 63 (1971), pp. 401-441; John Paul II, Encyclical *Laborem Exercens* (September 14, 1981): *AAS* 73 (1981), pp. 577-647. Also Pius XII delivered a radio message (June 1, 1941) for the fiftieth anniversary of the encyclical of Leo XIII: *AAS* 33 (1941), pp. 195-205.

fullness of the word revealed by Christ Jesus[3] and with the assistance of the Holy Spirit (cf. Jn 14:16, 26; 16:13-15), reads events as they unfold in the course of history. She thus seeks to lead people to respond, with the support also of rational reflection and of the human sciences, to their vocation as responsible builders of earthly society.

2. Part of this large body of social teaching is the distinguished Encyclical *Populorum Progressio*,[4] which my esteemed predecessor Paul VI published on March 26, 1967.

The enduring relevance of this Encyclical is easily recognized if we note the series of commemorations which took place during 1987 in various forms and in many parts of the ecclesiastical and civil world. For this same purpose, the Pontifical Commission *Iustitia et Pax* sent a circular letter to the Synods of the Oriental Catholic Churches and to the Episcopal Conferences, asking for ideas and suggestions on the best way to celebrate the Encyclical's anniversary, to enrich its teachings and, if need be, to update them. At the time of the twentieth anniversary, the same Commission organized a solemn commemoration in which I myself took part and gave the concluding address.[5] And now, also taking into account the replies to the above-mentioned circular letter, I consider it appropriate, at the close of the year 1987, to devote an Encyclical to the theme of *Populorum Progressio*.

3. In this way I wish principally to achieve *two objectives* of no little importance: on the one hand, to pay homage to this historic document of Paul VI and to its teaching; on the other hand, following in the footsteps of my esteemed predecessors in the See of Peter, to reaffirm the *continuity* of the social doctrine as well as its constant *renewal*. In effect, continuity and renewal are a proof of the *perennial value* of the teaching of the Church.

This twofold dimension is typical of her teaching in the social sphere. On the one hand it is *constant*, for it remains identical in its fundamental inspiration, in its "principles of reflection," in its "criteria of judgment," in its basic "directives for

3. Cf. Second Vatican Ecumenical Council, Dogmatic Constitution on Divine Revelation, *Dei Verbum*, n. 4.

4. Paul VI, Encyclical *Populorum Progressio* (March 26, 1967): *AAS* 59 (1967), pp. 257-299.

5. Cf. *L'Osservatore Romano*, May 25, 1987.

action,"[6] and above all in its vital link with the Gospel of the Lord. On the other hand, it is ever *new*, because it is subject to the necessary and opportune adaptations suggested by the changes in historical conditions and by the unceasing flow of the events which are the setting of the life of people and society.

4. I am convinced that the teachings of the Encyclical *Populorum Progressio*, addressed to the people and the society of the '60s, retain all their force as an *appeal to conscience* today in the last part of the '80s, in an effort to trace the major lines of the present world always within the context of the aim and inspiration of the "development of peoples," which are still very far from being exhausted. I therefore propose to extend the impact of that message by bringing it to bear, with its possible applications, upon the present historical moment, which is no less dramatic than that of twenty years ago.

As we well know, time maintains a constant and unchanging rhythm. Today however we have the impression that it is passing *ever more quickly*, especially by reason of the multiplication and complexity of the phenomena in the midst of which we live. Consequently, the *configuration of the world* in the course of the last twenty years, while preserving certain fundamental constants, has undergone notable changes and presents some totally new aspects.

The present period of time, on the eve of the third Christian millennium, is characterized by a widespread expectancy, rather like a new "Advent"[7] which to some extent touches everyone. It offers an opportunity to study the teachings of the Encyclical in greater detail and to see their possible future developments.

The aim of the present *reflection* is to emphasize, through a theological investigation of the present world, the need for a fuller and more nuanced concept of development, according to the suggestions contained in the Encyclical. Its aim is also to indicate some ways of putting it into effect.

---

6. Cf. Congregation for the Doctrine of the Faith, Instruction on Christian Freedom and Liberation, *Libertatis Conscientia* (March 22, 1986), 72: *AAS* 79 (1987), p. 586; Paul VI, Apostolic Letter *Octogesima Adveniens* (May 14, 1971), n. 4: *AAS* 63 (1971), pp. 403f.

7. Cf. Encyclical *Redemptoris Mater* (March 25, 1987), n. 3: *AAS* 79 (1987), pp. 363f.; Homily at the Mass of January 1, 1987: *L'Osservatore Romano*, January 2, 1987.

II. Originality of the Encyclical
Populorum Progressio

5. As soon as it appeared, the document of Pope Paul VI captured the attention of public opinion by reason of its *originality*. In a concrete manner and with great clarity, it was possible to identify the above mentioned characteristics of *continuity* and *renewal* within the Church's social doctrine. The intention of rediscovering numerous aspects of this teaching, through a careful rereading of the Encyclical, will therefore constitute the main thread of the present reflections.

But first I wish to say a few words about the *date* of publication: the year 1967. The very fact that Pope Paul VI chose to publish a *social Encyclical* in that year invites us to consider the document in relationship to the Second Vatican Ecumenical Council, which had ended on December 8, 1965.

6. We should see something more in this than simple chronological *proximity*. The Encyclical *Populorum Progressio* presents itself, in a certain way, as *a document which applies the teachings of the Council*. It not only makes continual reference to the texts of the Council,[8] but it also flows from the same concern of the Church which inspired the whole effort of the Council—and in a particular way the Pastoral Constitution *Gaudium et Spes*—to coordinate and develop a number of themes of her social teaching.

---

8. The Encyclical *Populorum Progressio* cites the documents of the Second Vatican Ecumenical Council nineteen times, and sixteen of the references are to the Pastoral Constitution on the Church in the Modern World, *Gaudium et Spes*.

6

We can therefore affirm that the Encyclical *Populorum Progressio* is a kind of response to the *Council's appeal* with which the Constitution *Gaudium et Spes* begins: "The joys and the hopes, the griefs and the anxieties of the people of this age, especially those who are poor or in any way afflicted, these too are the joys and hopes, the griefs and anxieties of the followers of Christ. Indeed, nothing genuinely human fails to raise an echo in their hearts."[9] These words express the *fundamental motive* inspiring the great document of the Council, which begins by noting the situation of *poverty* and of *underdevelopment* in which millions of human beings live.

This *poverty* and *underdevelopment* are, under another name, the "griefs and the anxieties" of today, of "especially those who are poor." Before this vast panorama of pain and suffering, the Council wished to suggest horizons of joy and hope. The Encyclical of Paul VI has the same purpose, in full fidelity to the inspiration of the Council.

7. There is also the *theme* of the Encyclical which, in keeping with the great tradition of the Church's social teaching, takes up again in a direct manner the *new exposition* and *rich synthesis* which the Council produced, notably in the Constitution *Gaudium et Spes*.

With regard to the content and themes once again set forth by the Encyclical, the following should be emphasized: the awareness of the duty of the Church, as "an expert in humanity," "to scrutinize the signs of the times and to interpret them in the light of the Gospel"[10]; the awareness, equally profound, of her mission of "service," a mission distinct from the function of the State, even when she is concerned with people's concrete situation[11]; the reference to the notorious inequalities in the situations of those same people[12]; the confirmation of the Council's teaching, a faithful echo of the centuries-old tradition of the Church regarding the "universal purpose of goods"[13]; the appreciation of the culture and the technological civilization which

---

9. *Gaudium et Spes*, n. 1.
10. *Ibid.*, n. 4; cf. *Populorum Progressio*, n. 13: *loc. cit.*, pp. 263, 264.
11. Cf. *Gaudium et Spes*, n. 3; *Populorum Progressio*, n. 13: *loc. cit.*, p. 264.
12. Cf. *Gaudium et Spes*, n. 63; *Populorum Progressio*, n. 9: *loc. cit.*, p. 269.
13. Cf. *Gaudium et Spes*, n. 69; *Populorum Progressio*, n. 22: *loc. cit.*, p. 269.

contribute to human liberation,[14] without failing to recognize their limits[15]; finally, on the specific theme of development, which is precisely the theme of the Encyclical, the insistence on the "most serious duty" incumbent on the more developed nations "to help the developing countries."[16] The same idea of development proposed by the Encyclical flows directly from the approach which the Pastoral Constitution takes to this problem.[17]

These and other explicit references to the Pastoral Constitution lead one to conclude that the Encyclical presents itself as an *application* of the Council's teaching in social matters to the specific problem of the *development* and the *underdevelopment of peoples*.

8. This brief analysis helps us to appreciate better the *originality* of the Encyclical, which can be stated in *three* points.

The *first* is constituted by the *very fact* of a document, issued by the highest authority of the Catholic Church and addressed both to the Church herself and "to all people of good will,"[18] on a matter which at first sight is solely *economic* and *social:* the *development* of peoples. The term "development" is taken from the vocabulary of the social and economic sciences. From this point of view, the Encyclical *Populorum Progressio* follows directly in the line of the Encyclical *Rerum Novarum*, which deals with the "condition of the workers."[19] Considered superficially, both themes could seem extraneous to the legitimate concern of the Church seen as a *religious institution*—and "development" even more so than the "condition of the workers."

In continuity with the Encyclical of Leo XIII, it must be recognized that the document of Paul VI possesses the merit of

---

14. Cf. *Gaudium et Spes*, n. 57; *Populorum Progressio*, n. 41: *loc. cit.*, p. 277.

15. Cf. *Gaudium et Spes*, n. 19; *Populorum Progressio*, n. 41: *loc. cit.*, pp. 277f.

16. Cf. *Gaudium et Spes*, n. 86; *Populorum Progressio*, n. 48: *loc. cit.*, p. 281.

17. Cf. *Gaudium et Spes*, n. 69; *Populorum Progressio*, nn. 14-21: *loc. cit.*, pp. 264-268.

18. Cf. the *Inscriptio* of the Encyclical *Populorum Progressio*: *loc. cit.*, p. 257.

19. The Encyclical *Rerum Novarum* of Leo XIII has as its principal subject "the condition of the workers": *Leonis XIII P. M. Acta*, XI, Romae 1892, p. 97.

having emphasized the *ethical* and *cultural character* of the problems connected with development, and likewise the legitimacy and necessity of the Church's intervention in this field.

In addition, the social doctrine of the Church has once more demonstrated its character as an *application* of the word of God to people's lives and the life of society, as well as to the earthly realities connected with them, offering "principles for reflection," "criteria of judgment" and "directives for action."[20] Here, in the document of Paul VI, one finds these three elements with a prevalently practical orientation, that is, directed towards *moral conduct*.

In consequence, when the Church concerns herself with the "development of peoples," she cannot be accused of going outside her own specific field of competence and, still less, outside the mandate received from the Lord.

9. The *second* point of *originality* of *Populorum Progressio* is shown by the *breadth of outlook* open to what is commonly called the "social question."

In fact, the Encyclical *Mater et Magistra* of Pope John XXIII had already entered into this wider outlook,[21] and the Council had echoed the same in the Constitution *Gaudium et Spes.*[22] However, the social teaching of the Church had not yet reached the point of affirming with such clarity that the social question has acquired a worldwide dimension,[23] nor had this affirmation and the accompanying analysis yet been made into a "directive for action," as Paul VI did in his Encyclical.

Such an explicit taking up of a position offers a *great wealth* of content, which it is appropriate to point out.

In the first place a *possible misunderstanding* has to be eliminated. Recognition that the "social question" has assumed a worldwide dimension does not at all mean that it has lost its *in-*

---

20. Cf. Congregation for the Doctrine of the Faith, Instruction on Christian Freedom and Liberation, *Libertatis Conscientia* (March 22, 1986), n. 72: *AAS* 79 (1987), p. 586; Paul VI, Apostolic Letter *Octogesima Adveniens* (May 14, 1971), n. 4: *AAS* 63 (1971), pp. 403f.

21. Cf. Encyclical *Mater et Magistra* (May 15, 1961): *AAS* 53 (1961), p. 440.

22. *Gaudium et Spes*, n. 63.

23. Cf. Encyclical *Populorum Progressio*, n. 3: *loc. cit.*, p. 258; cf. also *ibid.*, n. 9: *loc. cit.*, p. 261.

cisiveness or its national and local importance. On the contrary, it means that the problems in industrial enterprises or in the workers' and union movements of a particular country or region are not to be considered as isolated cases with no connection. On the contrary they depend more and more on the influence of factors beyond regional boundaries and national frontiers.

Unfortunately, from the economic point of view, the developing countries are much more numerous than the developed ones; the multitudes of human beings who lack the goods and services offered by development are *much more numerous* than those who possess them.

We are therefore faced with a serious problem of *unequal distribution* of the means of subsistence originally meant for everybody, and thus also an unequal distribution of the benefits deriving from them. And this happens not through the *fault* of the needy people, and even less through a sort of *inevitability* dependent on natural conditions or circumstances as a whole.

The Encyclical of Paul VI, in declaring that the social question has acquired worldwide dimensions, first of all points out a *moral fact*, one which has its foundation in an objective analysis of reality. In the words of the Encyclical itself, "each one must be conscious" of this fact,[24] precisely because it directly concerns the conscience, which is the source of moral decisions.

In this framework, the *originality* of the Encyclical consists not so much in the affirmation, historical in character, of the universality of the social question, but rather in the *moral evaluation* of this reality. Therefore political leaders, and citizens of rich countries considered as individuals, especially if they are Christians, have *the moral obligation*, according to the degree of each one's responsibility, to *take into consideration*, in personal decisions and decisions of government, this relationship of universality, this interdependence which exists between their conduct and the poverty and underdevelopment of so many millions of people. Pope Paul's Encyclical translates more succinctly the moral obligation as the "duty of solidarity"[25]; and this affirmation, even though many situations have changed in the world, has the same force and validity today as when it was written.

---

24. Cf. Encyclical *Populorum Progressio*, n. 3: *loc. cit.*, p. 258.
25. *Ibid.*, n. 48: *loc. cit.*, p. 281.

On the other hand, without departing from the lines of this moral vision, the *originality* of the Encyclical also consists in the basic insight that the *very concept* of development, if considered in the perspective of universal interdependence, changes notably. True development *cannot* consist in the simple accumulation of wealth and in the greater availability of goods and services, if this is gained at the expense of the development of the masses, and without due consideration for the social, cultural and spiritual dimensions of the human being.[26]

10. As a *third point*, the Encyclical provides a very original contribution to the social doctrine of the Church in its totality and to the very concept of development. This originality is recognizable in a phrase of the document's concluding paragraph, which can be considered as its summary, as well as its historic label: "Development is the new name for peace."[27]

In fact, if the social question has acquired a worldwide dimension, this is because *the demand for justice* can only be satisfied on that level. To ignore this demand could encourage the temptation among the victims of injustice to respond with violence, as happens at the origin of many wars. Peoples excluded from the fair distribution of the goods originally destined for all could ask themselves: why not respond with violence to those who first treat us with violence? And if the situation is examined in the light of the division of the world into ideological blocs—a division already existing in 1967—and in the light of the subsequent economic and political repercussions and dependencies, the danger is seen to be much greater.

The first consideration of the striking content of the Encyclical's historic phrase may be supplemented by a second consideration to which the document itself alludes[28]: how can one justify the fact that *huge sums of money*, which could and should be used for increasing the development of peoples, are instead utilized for the enrichment of individuals or groups, or assigned

---

26. Cf. Encyclical *Populorum Progressio*, n. 14: *loc. cit.*, p. 264: "Development cannot be limited to mere economic growth. In order to be authentic, it must be complete: integral, that is, it has to promote the good of every man and of the whole man."

27. *Ibid.*, n. 87: *loc. cit.*, p. 299.

28. Cf. *ibid.*, n. 53: *loc. cit.*, p. 283.

to the increase of stockpiles of weapons, both in developed countries and in the developing ones, thereby upsetting the real priorities? This is even more serious given the difficulties which often hinder the direct transfer of capital set aside for helping needy countries. If "development is the new name for peace," war and military preparations are the major enemy of the integral development of peoples.

In the light of this expression of Pope Paul VI, we are thus invited to re-examine the *concept of development*. This of course is not limited to merely satisfying material necessities through an increase of goods, while ignoring the sufferings of the many and making the selfishness of individuals and nations the principal motivation. As the Letter of St. James pointedly reminds us: "What causes wars, and what causes fightings among you? Is it not your passions that are at war in your members? You desire and do not have" (Js 4:1-2).

On the contrary, in a different world, ruled by concern for the *common good* of all humanity, or by concern for the "spiritual and human development of all" instead of by the quest for individual profit, peace would be *possible* as the result of a "more perfect justice among people."[29]

Also this new element of the Encyclical has a *permanent and contemporary value*, in view of the modern attitude which is so sensitive to the close link between respect for justice and the establishment of real peace.

---

29. Cf. Encyclical *Populorum Progressio*, n. 76: *loc. cit.*, p. 295.

III. Survey of the Contemporary World

11. In its own time *the fundamental teaching* of the Encyclical *Populorum Progressio* received great acclaim for its novel character. The social context in which we live today cannot be said to be completely *identical* to that of twenty years ago. For this reason, I now wish to conduct a brief review of some of the characteristics of today's world, in order to develop the teaching of Paul VI's Encyclical, once again from the point of view of the "development of peoples."

12. The *first fact* to note is that the *hopes for development*, at that time so lively, today appear very far from being realized.

In this regard, the Encyclical had no illusions. Its language, grave and at times dramatic, limited itself to stressing the seriousness of the situation and to bringing before the conscience of all the urgent obligation of contributing to its solution. In those years there was a *certain* widespread *optimism* about the possibility of overcoming, without excessive efforts, the economic backwardness of the poorer peoples, of providing them with infrastructures and assisting them in the process of industrialization.

In that historical context, over and above the efforts of each country, the United Nations Organization promoted consecutively *two decades of development*.[30] In fact, some measures, bilateral and multilateral, were taken with the aim of helping

---

30. The decades referred to are the years 1960-1970 and 1970-1980; the present decade is the third (1980-1990).

many nations, some of which had already been independent for
some time, and others—the majority—being States just born
from the process of decolonization. For her part, the Church felt
the duty to deepen her understanding of the problems posed by
the new situation, in the hope of supporting these efforts with
her religious and human inspiration, in order to give them a
"soul" and an effective impulse.

13. It cannot be said that these various religious, human,
economic and technical initiatives have been in vain, for they
have succeeded in achieving certain results. But in general,
taking into account the various factors, one cannot deny that the
present situation of the world, from the point of view of development, offers a *rather negative* impression.

For this reason, I wish to call attention to a number of *general
indicators*, without excluding other specific ones. Without going
into an analysis of figures and statistics, it is sufficient to face
squarely the reality of an *innumerable multitude of people*—children, adults and the elderly—in other words, real and unique
human persons, who are suffering under the intolerable burden
of poverty. There are many millions who are deprived of hope
due to the fact that, in many parts of the world, their situation
has noticeably worsened. Before these tragedies of total in-
digence and need, in which so many of *our brothers and sisters*
are living, it is the Lord Jesus himself who comes to question us
(cf. Mt 25:31-46).

14. The first *negative observation* to make is the persistence and
often the widening of the *gap* between the areas of the so-called
developed North and the developing South. This geographical
terminology is only indicative, since one cannot ignore the fact
that the frontiers of wealth and poverty intersect within the
societies themselves, whether developed or developing. In fact,
just as social inequalities down to the level of poverty exist in
rich countries, so, in parallel fashion, in the less developed countries one often sees manifestations of selfishness and a flaunting
of wealth which is as disconcerting as it is scandalous.

The abundance of goods and services available in some parts
of the world, particularly in the developed North, is matched in
the South by an unacceptable delay, and it is precisely in this
geopolitical area that the major part of the human race lives.

Looking at all the various sectors—the production and distribution of foodstuffs, hygiene, health and housing, availability of drinking water, working conditions (especially for women), life expectancy and other economic and social indicators—the general picture is a disappointing one, both considered in itself and in relation to the corresponding data of the more developed countries. The word "gap" returns spontaneously to mind.

Perhaps this is not the appropriate word for indicating the true reality, since it could give the impression of a *stationary* phenomenon. This is not the case. The *pace of progress* in the developed and developing countries in recent years has differed, and this serves to widen the distances. Thus the developing countries, especially the poorest of them, find themselves in a situation of very serious delay.

We must also add the *differences of culture* and *value systems* between the various population groups, differences which do not always match the degree of *economic development*, but which help to create distances. These are elements and aspects which render *the social question much more complex*, precisely because this question has assumed a universal dimension.

As we observe the various parts of the world separated by this widening gap, and note that each of these parts seems to follow its own path with its own achievements, we can understand the current usage which speaks of different worlds within our *one world:* the First World, the Second World, the Third World and at times the Fourth World.[31] Such expressions, which obviously do not claim to classify exhaustively all countries, are significant: they are a sign of a widespread sense that the *unity of the world*, that is, *the unity of the human race*, is seriously compromised. Such phraseology, beyond its more or less objective value, undoubtedly conceals a *moral content*, before which the Church, which is a "sacrament or sign and instrument . . . of the unity of the whole human race,"[32] cannot remain indifferent.

15. However, the picture just given would be incomplete if

---

31. The expression "Fourth World" is used not just occasionally for the so-called *less advanced* countries, but also and especially for the bands of great or extreme poverty in countries of medium and high income.

32. Second Vatican Ecumenical Council, Dogmatic Constitution on the Church, *Lumen Gentium*, n. 1.

one failed to add to the "economic and social indices" of underdevelopment other indices which are equally negative and
indeed even more disturbing, beginning with the cultural level.
These are *illiteracy*, the difficulty or impossibility of obtaining
higher education, the inability to share in the *building of one's own
nation*, the *various forms of exploitation* and of economic, social,
political and even religious *oppression of* the individual and his
or her rights, *discrimination of every type*, especially the excep-
tionally odious form based on difference of race. If some of these
scourges are noted with regret in areas of the more developed
North, they are undoubtedly more frequent, more lasting and
more difficult to root out in the developing and less advanced
countries.

It should be noted that in today's world, among other rights,
the right of economic initiative is often suppressed. Yet it is a right
which is important not only for the individual but also for the
common good. Experience shows us that the denial of this right,
or its limitation in the name of an alleged "equality" of everyone in society, diminishes, or in practice absolutely destroys the
spirit of initiative, that is to say *the creative subjectivity of the citizen*. As a consequence, there arises, not so much a true equality
as a "leveling down." In the place of creative initiative there appears passivity, dependence and submission to the bureaucratic
apparatus which, as the only "ordering" and "decision-making"
body—if not also the "owner"—of the entire totality of goods
and the means of production, puts everyone in a position of almost absolute dependence, which is similar to the traditional
dependence of the worker-proletarian in capitalism. This provokes a sense of frustration or desperation and predisposes
people to opt out of national life, impelling many to emigrate
and also favoring a form of "psychological" emigration.

Such a situation has its consequences also from the point of
view of the "rights of the individual nations." In fact, it often happens that a nation is deprived of its subjectivity, that is to say the
"sovereignty" which is its right, in its economic, political-social
and in a certain way cultural significance, since in a national community all these dimensions of life are bound together.

It must also be restated that no social group, for example a
political party, has the right to usurp the role of sole leader, since
this brings about the destruction of the true subjectivity of

society and of the individual citizens, as happens in every form of totalitarianism. In this situation the individual and the people become "objects," in spite of all declarations to the contrary and verbal assurances.

We should add here that in today's world there are many other *forms of poverty*. For are there not certain privations or deprivations which deserve this name? The denial or the limitation of human rights—as for example the right to religious freedom, the right to share in the building of society, the freedom to organize and to form unions, or to take initiatives in economic matters—do these not impoverish the human person as much as, if not more than, the deprivation of material goods? And is development which does not take into account the full affirmation of these rights really development on the human level?

In brief, modern underdevelopment is not only economic but also cultural, political and simply human, as was indicated twenty years ago by the Encyclical *Populorum Progressio*. Hence at this point we have to ask ourselves if the sad reality of today might not be, at least in part, the result of a *too narrow idea* of development, that is, a mainly economic one.

16. It should be noted that in spite of the praiseworthy efforts made in the last two decades by the more developed or developing nations and the international organizations to find a way out of the situation, or at least to remedy some of its symptoms, the conditions have become *notably worse*.

Responsibility for this deterioration is due to various causes. Notable among them are undoubtedly grave instances of omissions on the part of the developing nations themselves, and especially on the part of those holding economic and political power. Nor can we pretend not to see the responsibility of the developed nations, which have not always, at least in due measure, felt the duty to help countries separated from the affluent world to which they themselves belong.

Moreover, one must denounce the existence of economic, financial and social *mechanisms* which, although they are manipulated by people, often function almost automatically, thus accentuating the situation of wealth for some and poverty for the rest. These mechanisms, which are maneuvered directly or indirectly by the more developed countries, by their very functioning favor the interests of the people manipulating them. But in the end they suffocate or condition the economies of the less developed countries. Later on these mechanisms will have to be subjected to a careful analysis under the ethical-moral aspect.

Populorum Progressio already foresaw the possibility that under such systems the wealth of the rich would increase and the poverty of the poor would remain.[33] A proof of this forecast has been the appearance of the so-called Fourth World.

17. However much society worldwide shows signs of fragmentation, expressed in the conventional names First, Second, Third and even Fourth World, their *interdependence* remains close. When this interdependence is separated from its ethical requirements, it has *disastrous consequences* for the weakest. Indeed, as a result of a sort of internal dynamic and under the impulse of mechanisms which can only be called perverse, this *interdependence* triggers *negative effects* even in the rich countries. It is precisely within these countries that one encounters, though on a lesser scale, the *more specific manifestations* of underdevelopment. Thus it should be obvious that development either becomes shared in *common* by every part of the world or it undergoes a *process of regression* even in zones marked by constant progress. This tells us a great deal about the nature of *authentic* development: either *all* the nations of the world participate, or it will not be true development.

Among the *specific signs* of underdevelopment which increasingly affect the developed countries also, there are two in particular that reveal a tragic situation. The *first* is the *housing crisis*. During this International Year of the Homeless proclaimed by the United Nations, attention is focused on the millions of human beings lacking adequate housing or with no housing at all, in order to awaken everyone's conscience and to find a solution to this serious problem with its negative consequences for the individual, the family and society.[34]

The lack of housing is being experienced *universally* and is

---

33. Encyclical *Populorum Progressio*, n. 33: *loc. cit.*, p. 273.

34. It should be noted that the Holy See associated itself with the celebration of this International Year with a special Document issued by the Pontifical Commission *Iustitia et Pax* entitled: "What Have You Done to Your Homeless Brother?" *The Church and the Housing Problem* (December 27, 1987).

due in large measure to the growing phenomenon of urbanization.[35] Even the most highly developed peoples present the sad spectacle of individuals and families literally struggling to survive, without a *roof* over their heads or with a roof *so inadequate* as to constitute no roof at all.

The lack of housing, an extremely serious problem in itself, should be seen as a sign and summing-up of a whole series of shortcomings: economic, social, cultural or simply human in nature. Given the extent of the problem, we should need little convincing of how far we are from an authentic development of peoples.

18. *Another indicator* common to the vast majority of nations is the phenomenon of *unemployment* and *underemployment*.

Everyone recognizes the *reality* and *growing seriousness* of this problem in the industrialized countries.[36] While it is alarming in the developing countries, with their high rate of population growth and their large numbers of young people, in the countries of high economic development the *sources of work* seem to be shrinking, and thus the opportunities for employment are decreasing rather than increasing.

This phenomenon too, with its series of negative consequences for individuals and for society, ranging from humiliation to the loss of that self-respect which every man and woman should have, prompts us to question seriously the type of development which has been followed over the past twenty years. Here the words of the Encyclical *Laborem Exercens* are extremely appropriate: "It must be stressed that the constitutive element in the *progress* and also the most adequate *way to verify it* in a spirit of justice and peace, which the Church proclaims and for which she does not cease to pray . . . is *the continual reappraisal of man's work*, both in the aspect of its objective finality and in the aspect of the dignity of the subject of all work, that is to say, man." On the other hand, "we cannot fail to be struck by *a dis-*

---

35. Cf. Paul VI, Apostolic Letter *Octogesima Adveniens* (May 14, 1971), nn. 8-9: *AAS* 63 (1971), pp. 406-408.

36. A recent United Nations publication entitled *World Economic Survey 1987* provides the most recent data (cf. pp. 8-9). The percentage of unemployed in the developed countries with a market economy jumped from 3% of the work force in 1970 to 8% in 1986. It now amounts to 29 million people.

concerting fact of immense proportions: the fact that . . . there are
huge numbers of people who are unemployed . . . a fact that
without any doubt demonstrates that both within the individual
political communities and in their relationships on the continental and world level there is something wrong with the organization of work and employment, precisely at the most critical
and socially most important point."[37]

This second phenomenon, like the previous one, because it is
universal in character and tends to *proliferate*, is a very telling
negative sign of the state and the quality of the development of
peoples which we see today.

19. A *third phenomenon,* likewise characteristic of the most recent period, even though it is not met with everywhere, is
without doubt equally indicative of the *interdependence* between
developed and less developed countries. It is the question of the
international debt, concerning which the Pontifical Commission
Iustitia et Pax has issued a document.[38]

At this point one cannot ignore the *close connection* between
a problem of this kind—the growing seriousness of which was
already foreseen in *Populorum Progressio*[39]—and the question of
the development of peoples.

The reason which prompted the developing peoples to accept
the offer of abundantly available capital was the hope of being
able to invest it in development projects. Thus the availability of
capital and the fact of accepting it as a loan can be considered a
contribution to development, something desirable and legitimate
in itself, even though perhaps imprudent and occasionally hasty.

Circumstances have changed, both within the debtor nations
and in the international financial market; the instrument chosen

---

37. Encyclical *Laborem Exercens* (September 14, 1981), n. 18: *AAS* 73
(1981), pp. 624-625.

38. *At the Service of the Human Community: An Ethical Approach to the International Debt Question* (December 27, 1986).

39. Encyclical *Populorum Progressio,* n. 54; *loc. cit.,* pp. 283f.: "Developing countries will thus no longer risk being overwhelmed by debts
whose repayment swallows up the greater part of their gains. Rates of interest and time for repayment of the loan could be so arranged as not to
be too great a burden on either party, taking into account free gifts, inter-
est-free or low-interest loans, and the time needed for liquidating the
debts."

to make a contribution to development has turned into a *counter-productive mechanism*. This is because the debtor nations, in order to service their debt, find themselves obliged to export the capital needed for improving or at least maintaining their standard of living. It is also because, for the same reason, they are unable to obtain new and equally essential financing.

Through this mechanism, the means intended for the development of peoples has turned into a *brake* upon development instead, and indeed in some cases has even *aggravated underdevelopment*.

As the recent document of the Pontifical Commission *Iustitia et Pax* states,[40] these observations should make us reflect on the *ethical character* of the interdependence of peoples. And along similar lines, they should make us reflect on the requirements and conditions, equally inspired by ethical principles, for cooperation in development.

20. If at this point we examine the *reasons* for this serious delay in the process of development, a delay which has occurred contrary to the indications of the Encyclical *Populorum Progressio*, which had raised such great hopes, our attention is especially drawn to the *political* causes of today's situation.

Faced with a combination of factors which are undoubtedly complex, we cannot hope to achieve a comprehensive analysis here. However, we cannot ignore a striking fact about the *political picture* since the Second World War, a fact which has considerable impact on the forward movement of the development of peoples.

I am referring to the *existence of two opposing blocs*, commonly known as the East and the West. The reason for this description is not purely political but is also, as the expression goes, *geopolitical*. Each of the two blocs tends to assimilate or gather around it other countries or groups of countries, to different degrees of adherence or participation.

The opposition is first of all *political*, inasmuch as each bloc identifies itself with a system of organizing society and exercising power which presents itself as an alternative to the other.

---

40. Cf. "Presentation" of the document *At the Service of the Human Community: An Ethical Approach to the International Debt Question* (December 27, 1986).

The political opposition, in turn, takes its origin from a deeper opposition which is *ideological* in nature.

In the West there exists a system which is historically inspired by the principles of the *liberal capitalism* which developed with industrialization during the last century. In the East there exists a system inspired by the *Marxist collectivism* which sprang from an interpretation of the condition of the proletarian classes made in the light of a particular reading of history. Each of the two ideologies, on the basis of two very different visions of man and of his freedom and social role, has proposed and still promotes, on the economic level, antithetical forms of the organization of labor and of the structures of ownership, especially with regard to the so-called means of production.

It was inevitable that by developing antagonistic systems and centers of power, each with its own forms of propaganda and indoctrination, the *ideological opposition* should evolve into a growing *military opposition* and give rise to two blocs of armed forces, each suspicious and fearful of the other's domination.

International relations, in turn, could not fail to feel the effects of this "logic of blocs" and of the respective "spheres of influence." The tension between the two blocs which began at the end of the Second World War has dominated the whole of the subsequent forty years. Sometimes it has taken the form of *"cold war,"* sometimes of *"wars by proxy,"* through the manipulation of local conflicts, and sometimes it has kept people's minds in suspense and anguish by the threat of an *open and total* war.

Although at the present time this danger seems to have receded, yet without completely disappearing, and even though an initial agreement has been reached on the destruction of one type of nuclear weapon, the existence and opposition of the blocs continue to be a real and worrying fact which still colors the world picture.

21. This happens with particularly negative effects in international relations which concern the developing countries. For as we know the tension *between East and West* is not in itself an opposition between two different *levels* of development but rather between two *concepts* of the development of individuals and peoples, both concepts being imperfect and in need of radical correction. This opposition is transferred to the developing countries themselves, and thus helps to widen the gap already

existing on the economic level between *North and South* and which results from the distance between the two *worlds:* the more developed one and the less developed one.

This is one of the reasons why the Church's social doctrine adopts a critical attitude towards both liberal capitalism and Marxist collectivism. For from the point of view of development the question naturally arises: in what way and to what extent are these two systems capable of changes and updatings such as to favor or promote a true and integral development of individuals and peoples in modern society? In fact, these changes and updatings are urgent and essential for the cause of a development common to all.

Countries which have recently achieved independence, and which are trying to establish a cultural and political identity of their own, and need effective and impartial aid from all the richer and more developed countries, find themselves involved in, and sometimes overwhelmed by, ideological conflicts, which inevitably create internal divisions, to the extent in some cases of provoking full civil war. This is also because investments and aid for development are often diverted from their proper purpose and in opposition to the interests of the countries which ought to benefit from them. Many of these countries are becoming more and more aware of the danger of falling victim to a form of neo-colonialism and are trying to escape from it. It is this awareness which in spite of difficulties, uncertainties and at times contradictions gave rise to the *International Movement of Non-Aligned Nations*, which, in its positive aspect, would like to affirm in an effective way the right of every people to its own identity, independence and security, as well as the right to share, on a basis of equality and solidarity, in the goods intended for all.

22. In the light of these considerations, we easily arrive at a clearer picture of the last twenty years and a better understanding of the conflicts in the northern hemisphere, namely between East and West, as an important cause of the retardation or stagnation of the South.

The developing countries, instead of becoming *autonomous nations* concerned with their own progress towards a just sharing in the goods and services meant for all, become parts of a machine, cogs on a gigantic wheel. This is often true also in the

field of social communications, which, being run by centers
mostly in the northern hemisphere, do not always give due consideration to the priorities and problems of such countries or respect their cultural make-up. They frequently impose a distorted vision of life and of man and thus fail to respond to the
demands of true development.

Each of the two *blocs* harbors in its own way a tendency
towards *imperialism*, as it is usually called, or towards forms of
new-colonialism: an easy temptation to which they frequently
succumb, as history, including recent history, teaches.

It is this abnormal situation, the result of a war and of an unacceptably exaggerated concern *for security*, which deadens the
impulse towards united cooperation by all for the common good
of the human race, to the detriment especially of peaceful
peoples who are impeded from their rightful access to the goods
meant for all.

Seen in this way, the present division of the world is a *direct
obstacle* to the real transformation of the conditions of underdevelopment in the developing and less advanced countries.
However, peoples do not always resign themselves to their fate.
Furthermore, the very needs of an economy stifled by military
expenditure and by bureaucracy and intrinsic inefficiency now
seem to favor processes which might mitigate the existing opposition and make it easier to begin a fruitful dialogue and
genuine collaboration for peace.

23. The statement in the Encyclical *Populorum Progressio* that
the resources and investments devoted to arms production
ought to be used to alleviate the misery of impoverished
peoples[41] makes more urgent the appeal to overcome the opposition between the two blocs.

Today, the reality is that these resources are used to enable
each of the two blocs to overtake the other and thus guarantee
its own security. Nations which historically, economically and
politically have the possibility of playing a leadership role are
prevented by this fundamentally flawed distortion from ade-
quately fulfilling their duty of solidarity for the benefit of
peoples which aspire to full development.

It is timely to mention—and it is no exaggeration—that a

---

41. Cf. Encyclical *Populorum Progressio*, n. 53: *loc. cit.*, p. 283.

leadership role among nations can only be justified by the possibility and willingness to contribute widely and generously to the common good.

If a nation were to succumb more or less deliberately to the temptation to close in upon itself and failed to meet the responsibilities following from its superior position in the community of nations, it *would fall seriously short* of its clear ethical duty. This is readily apparent in the circumstances of history, where believers discern the dispositions of Divine Providence, ready to make use of the nations for the realization of its plans, so as to render "vain the designs of the peoples" (cf. Ps 33[23]:10).

When the West gives the impression of abandoning itself to forms of growing and selfish isolation, and the East in its turn seems to ignore for questionable reasons its duty to cooperate in the task of alleviating human misery, then we are up against not only a betrayal of humanity's legitimate expectations—a betrayal that is a harbinger of unforeseeable consequences—but also a real desertion of a moral obligation.

24. If arms production is a serious disorder in the present world with regard to true human needs and the employment of the means capable of satisfying those needs, *the arms trade* is equally to blame. Indeed, with reference to the latter it must be added that the *moral judgment is even more severe.* As we all know, this is a trade without frontiers, capable of crossing even the barriers of the blocs. It knows how to overcome the division between East and West, and above all the one between North and South, to the point—and this is more serious—of pushing its way into the *different sections* which make up the southern hemisphere. We are thus confronted with a strange phenomenon: while economic aid and development plans meet with the obstacle of insuperable ideological barriers, and with tariff and trade barriers, *arms* of whatever origin circulate with almost total freedom all over the world. And as the recent document of the Pontifical Commission *Iustitia et Pax* on the international debt points out,[42] everyone knows that in certain cases the capital lent by the developed world has been used in the underdeveloped world to buy weapons.

---

42. *At the Service of the Human Community: An Ethical Approach to the International Debt Question* (December 27, 1986), III, 2, 1.

If to all this we add the *tremendous* and universally acknowledged *danger* represented by *atomic weapons* stockpiled on an incredible scale, the logical conclusion seems to be this: in today's
world, including the world of economics, the prevailing picture
is one destined to lead us more quickly *towards death* rather than
one of concern for *true development* which would lead all towards
a "more human" life, as envisaged by the Encyclical *Populorum
Progressio*.[43]

The consequences of this state of affairs are to be seen in the
festering of a *wound* which typifies and reveals the imbalances
and conflicts of the modern world: *the millions of refugees* whom
war, natural calamities, persecution and discrimination of every
kind have deprived of home, employment, family and home-
land. The tragedy of these multitudes is reflected in the hope-
less faces of men, women and children who can no longer find
a home in a divided and inhospitable world.

Nor may we close our eyes to another painful wound in
today's world: the phenomenon of *terrorism*, understood as the
intention to kill people and destroy property indiscriminately,
and to create a climate of terror and insecurity, often including
the taking of hostages. Even when some ideology or the desire
to create a better society is adduced as the motivation for this
inhuman behavior, acts of terrorism are never justifiable. Even
less so when, as happens today, such decisions and such actions, which at times lead to real massacres, and to the abduc-
tion of innocent people who have nothing to do with the conflicts, claim to have a propaganda purpose for furthering a
cause. It is still worse when they are an end in themselves, so
that murder is committed merely for the sake of killing. In the
face of such horror and suffering, the words I spoke some years
ago are still true, and I wish to repeat them again: "What Christianity forbids is to seek solutions . . . by the ways of hatred, by
the murdering of defenseless people, by the methods of terrorism."[44]

25. At this point something must be said about the *demographic problem* and the way it is spoken of today, following what

---

43. Cf. Encyclical *Populorum Progressio*, nn. 20-21: *loc. cit.*, pp. 267f.

44. Address at Drogheda, Ireland (September 29, 1979), n. 5: *AAS* 71
(1979), II, p. 1079.

Paul VI said in his Encyclical[45] and what I myself stated at length in the Apostolic Exhortation *Familiaris Consortio*.[46]

One cannot deny the existence, especially in the southern hemisphere, of a demographic problem which creates difficulties for development. One must immediately add that in the northern hemisphere the nature of this problem is reversed: here, the cause for concern is the *drop in the birthrate*, with repercussions on the aging of the population, unable even to renew itself biologically. In itself, this is a phenomenon capable of hindering development. Just as it is incorrect to say that such difficulties stem solely from demographic growth, neither is it proved that *all* demographic growth is incompatible with orderly development.

On the other hand, it is very alarming to see governments in many countries launching *systematic campaigns* against birth, contrary not only to the cultural and religious identity of the countries themselves but also contrary to the nature of true development. It often happens that these campaigns are the result of pressure and financing coming from abroad, and in some cases they are made a condition for the granting of financial and economic aid and assistance. In any event, there is an *absolute lack of respect* for the freedom of choice of the parties involved, men and women often subjected to intolerable pressures, including economic ones, in order to force them to submit to this new form of oppression. It is the poorest populations which suffer such mistreatment, and this sometimes leads to a tendency towards a form of racism, or the promotion of certain equally racist forms of eugenics.

This fact too, which deserves the most forceful condemnation, is a *sign* of an erroneous and perverse *idea* of true human development.

26. This mainly negative overview of the *actual situation* of development in the contemporary world would be incomplete without a mention of the coexistence of *positive aspects*.

The *first* positive note is the *full awareness* among large numbers of men and women of their own dignity and of that of every

---

45. Cf. Encyclical *Populorum Progressio*, n. 37: *loc. cit.*, pp. 275f.

46. Cf. Apostolic Exhortation *Familiaris Consortio* (November 22, 1981), especially in n. 30: *AAS* 74 (1982), pp. 115-117.

human being. This awareness is expressed, for example, in the more *lively concern* that *human rights should be respected*, and in the more vigorous rejection of their violation. One sign of this is the number of recently established private associations, some worldwide in membership, almost all of them devoted to monitoring with great care and commendable objectivity what is happening *internationally* in this sensitive field.

At this level one must acknowledge the *influence* exercised by the *Declaration of Human Rights*, promulgated some forty years ago by the United Nations Organization. Its very existence and gradual acceptance by the international community are signs of a growing awareness. The same is to be said, still in the field of human rights, of other juridical instruments issued by the United Nations Organization or other international organizations.[47]

The awareness under discussion applies not only to *individuals* but also to *nations* and *peoples*, which, as entities having a specific cultural identity, are particularly sensitive to the preservation, free exercise and promotion of their precious heritage.

At the same time, in a world divided and beset by every type of conflict, the *conviction* is growing of a radical *interdependence* and consequently of the need for a solidarity which will take up interdependence and transfer it to the moral plane. Today perhaps more than in the past, people are realizing that they are linked together by a *common destiny*, which is to be constructed together, if catastrophe for all is to be avoided. From the depth of anguish, fear and escapist phenomena like drugs, *typical of the contemporary world*, the idea is slowly emerging that the good to which we are all called and the happiness to which we aspire cannot be obtained without an *effort and commitment on the part of all*, nobody excluded, and the consequent renouncing of personal selfishness.

Also to be mentioned here, as a sign of *respect for life*—despite all the temptations to destroy it by abortion and euthanasia—is a *concomitant concern* for peace, together with an awareness that peace is *indivisible*. It is either *for all* or *for none*. It demands an ever greater degree of rigorous respect for *justice* and consequently a fair distribution of the results of true development.[48]

---

47. Cf. Human Rights: Collection of International Instruments, United Nations, New York, 1983; John Paul II, Encyclical *Redemptor Hominis* (March 4, 1979), n. 17: *AAS* 71 (1979), p. 296.

48. Cf. Second Vatican Ecumenical Council, Pastoral Constitution on

Among today's *positive signs* we must also mention a greater realization of the limits of available resources, and of the need to respect the integrity and the cycles of nature and to take them into account when planning for development, rather than sacrificing them to certain demagogic ideas about the latter. Today this is called *ecological concern*.

It is also right to acknowledge the generous commitment of statesmen, politicians, economists, trade unionists, people of science and international officials—many of them inspired by religious faith—who at no small personal sacrifice try to resolve the world's ills and who give of themselves in every way so as to ensure that an every increasing number of people may enjoy the benefits of peace and a quality of life worthy of the name.

The great *international organizations*, and a number of the regional organizations, *contribute* to this *in no small measure*. Their united efforts make possible more effective action.

It is also through these contributions that some Third World countries, despite the burden of many negative factors, have succeeded in reaching a *certain self-sufficiency in food,* or a degree of industrialization which makes it possible to survive with dignity and to guarantee sources of employment for the active population.

Thus, *all is not negative* in the contemporary world, nor would it be, for the Heavenly Father's providence lovingly watches over even our daily cares (cf. Mt 6:25-32; 10:23-31; Lk 12:6-7, 22-30). Indeed, the positive values which we have mentioned testify to a new moral concern, particularly with respect to the great human problems such as development and peace.

This fact prompts me to turn my thoughts to the *true nature* of the development of peoples, along the lines of the Encyclical which we are commemorating, and as a mark of respect for its teaching.

---

the Church in the Modern World, *Gaudium et Spes*, n. 78; Paul VI, Encyclical *Populorum Progressio*, n. 76: *loc. cit.*, pp. 294f.: "To wage war on misery and to struggle against injustice is to promote, along with improved conditions, the human and spiritual progress of all men, and therefore the common good of humanity . . . peace is something that is built up day after day, in the pursuit of an order intended by God, which implies a more perfect form of justice among men."

IV. Authentic Human Development

27. The examination which the Encyclical invites us to make of the contemporary world leads us to note in the first place that development *is not* a straightforward process, *as it were automatic* and *in itself limitless,* as though, given certain conditions, the human race were able to progress rapidly towards an undefined perfection of some kind.[49]

Such an idea—linked to a notion of "progress" with philosophical connotations deriving from the Enlightenment, rather than to the notion of "development"[50] which is used in a specifically economic and social sense—now seems to be seriously called into doubt, particularly since the tragic experience of the two world wars, the planned and partly achieved destruction of whole peoples, and the looming atomic peril. A naive *mechanistic optimism* has been replaced by a well-founded anxiety for the fate of humanity.

28. At the same time, however, the *"economic"* concept itself, linked to the word development, has entered into crisis. In fact there is a better understanding today that the *mere accumulation* of goods and services, even for the benefit of the majority, is not

---

49. Cf. Apostolic Exhortation *Familiaris Consortio* (November 22, 1981), n. 6: *AAS* 74 (1982), p. 88: ". . . history is not simply a fixed progression toward what is better, but rather an event of freedom, and even a struggle between freedoms. . . ."

50. For this reason the word "development" was used in the Encyclical rather than the word "progress," but with an attempt to give the word "development" its fullest meaning.

enough for the realization of human happiness. Nor, in consequence, does the availability of the many *real benefits* provided in recent times by science and technology, including the computer sciences, bring freedom from every form of slavery. On the contrary, the experience of recent years shows that unless all the considerable body of resources and potential at man's disposal is guided by a *moral understanding* and by an orientation towards the true good of the human race, it easily turns against man to oppress him.

A *disconcerting conclusion* about the most recent period should serve to enlighten us: side-by-side with the miseries of underdevelopment, themselves unacceptable, we find ourselves up against a form of *superdevelopment,* equally inadmissible, because like the former it is contrary to what is good and to true happiness. This superdevelopment, which consists in an *excessive* availability of every kind of material goods for the benefit of certain social groups, easily makes people slaves of "possession" and of immediate gratification, with no other horizon than the multiplication or continual replacement of the things already owned with others still better. This is the so-called civilization of "consumption" or "consumerism," which involves so much "throwing-away" and "waste." An object already owned but now superseded by something better is discarded, with no thought of its possible lasting value in itself, nor of some other human being who is poorer.

All of us experience firsthand the sad effects of this blind submission to pure consumerism: in the first place a crass materialism, and at the same time a *radical dissatisfaction,* because one quickly learns—unless one is shielded from the flood of publicity and the ceaseless and tempting offers of products—that the more one possesses the more one wants, while deeper aspirations remain unsatisfied and perhaps even stifled.

The Encyclical of Pope Paul VI pointed out the difference, so often emphasized today, between "having" and "being,"[51]

---

51. Encyclical *Populorum Progressio,* n. 19: *loc. cit.,* pp. 266f.: "Increased possession is not the ultimate goal of nations or of individuals. All growth is ambivalent. . . . The exclusive pursuit of possessions thus becomes an obstacle to individual fulfillment and to man's true greatness . . . both for nations and for individual men, avarice is the most evident form of moral

which had been expressed earlier in precise words by the Second Vatican Council.[52] To "have" objects and goods does not in itself perfect the human subject, unless it contributes to the maturing and enrichment of that subject's "being," that is to say unless it contributes to the realization of the human vocation as such.

Of course, the difference between "being" and "having," the danger inherent in a mere multiplication or replacement of things possessed compared to the value of "being," need not turn into a *contradiction*. One of the greatest injustices in the contemporary world consists precisely in this: that the ones who possess much are relatively *few* and those who possess almost nothing are *many*. It is the injustice of the poor distribution of the goods and services originally intended for all.

This then is the picture: there are some people—the few who possess much—who do not really succeed in "being" because, through a reversal of the hierarchy of values, they are hindered by the cult of "having"; and there are others—the many who have little or nothing—who do not succeed in realizing their basic human vocation because they are deprived of essential goods.

The evil does not consist in "having" as such, but in possessing without regard for the *quality* and the *ordered hierarchy* of the goods one has. *Quality and hierarchy* arise from the subordination of goods and their availability to man's "being" and his true vocation.

This shows that although *development* has a *necessary economic dimension*, since it must supply the greatest possible number of the world's inhabitants with an availability of goods essential for them "to be," it is not limited to that dimension. If it is limited to this, then it turns against those whom it is meant to benefit.

The characteristics of full development, one which is "more human" and able to sustain itself at the level of the true voca-

---

underdevelopment"; cf. also Paul VI, Apostolic Letter *Octogesima Adveniens* (May 14, 1971), n. 9: *AAS* 63 (1971), pp. 407f.

52. Cf. Pastoral Constitution on the Church in the Modern World, *Gaudium et Spes*, n. 35: Paul VI, Address to the Diplomatic Corps (January 7, 1965): *AAS* 57 (1965), p. 232.

tion of men and women without denying economic requirements, were described by Paul VI.[53]

29. Development which is not only economic must be
measured and oriented according to the reality and vocation of
man seen in his totality, namely, according to his *interior dimension*. There is no doubt that he needs created goods and the products of industry, which is constantly being enriched by scientific
and technological progress. And the ever greater availability of
material goods not only meets needs but also opens new horl-
zons. The danger of the misuse of material goods and the appearance of artificial needs should in no way hinder the regard
we have for the new goods and resources placed at our disposal
and the use we make of them. On the contrary, we must see them
as a gift from God and as a response to the human vocation,
which is fully realized in Christ.

However, in trying to achieve true development we must
never lose sight of that *dimension* which is in the *specific nature*
of man, who has been created by God in his image and likeness
(cf. Gen 1:26). It is a bodily and a spiritual nature, symbolized
in the second creation account by the two elements: the *earth*,
from which God forms man's body, and the *breath of life* which
he breathes into man's nostrils (cf. Gen 2:7).

Thus man comes to have a certain affinity with other creatures: he is called to use them, and to be involved with them. As
the Genesis account says (cf. Gen 2:15), he is placed in the garden with the duty of cultivating and watching over it, being superior to the other creatures placed by God under his dominion
(cf. Gen 1:25-26). But at the same time man must remain subject
to the will of God, who imposes limits upon his use and dominion over things (cf. Gen 2:16-17), just as he promises him immortality (cf. Gen 2:9; Wis 2:23). Thus man, being the image of God,
has a true affinity with him too.

On the basis of this teaching, development cannot consist
only in the use, dominion over and *indiscriminate* possession of
created things and the products of human industry, but rather
in *subordinating* the possession, dominion and use to man's
divine likeness and to his vocation to immortality. This is the

---

53. Cf. Encyclical Letter *Populorum Progressio*, nn. 20-21: *loc. cit.*, pp.
267f.

transcendent reality of the human being, a reality which is seen
to be shared from the beginning by a couple, a man and a woman
(cf. Gen 1:27), and is therefore fundamentally social.

30. According to Sacred Scripture therefore, the notion of development is not only "lay" or "profane," but it is also seen to
be, while having a socio-economic dimension of its own, the
modern expression of an essential dimension of man's vocation.

The fact is that man was not created, so to speak, immobile
and static. The first portrayal of him, as given in the Bible, certainly presents him as a *creature* and *image, defined* in his deepest reality by the *origin* and *affinity* that constitute him. But all
this plants within the human being—man and woman—the
seed and the *requirement* of a special task to be accomplished by
each individually and by them as a couple. The task is "to have
dominion" over the other created beings, "to cultivate the garden." This is to be accomplished within the framework of *obedience* to the divine law and therefore with respect for the image
received, the image which is the clear foundation of the power
of dominion recognized as belonging to man as the means to his
perfection (cf. Gen 1:26-30; 2:15-16; Wis 9:2-3).

When man disobeys God and refuses to submit to his rule,
nature rebels against him and no longer recognizes him as its
"master," for he has tarnished the divine image in himself. The
claim to ownership and use of created things remains still valid,
but after sin its exercise becomes difficult and full of suffering
(cf. Gen 3:17-19).

In fact, the following chapter of Genesis shows us that the de-
scendants of Cain build "a city," engage in sheep farming, practice the arts (music) and technical skills (metallurgy); while at
the same time people began to "call upon the name of the Lord"
(cf. Gen 4:17-26).

The story of the human race described by Sacred Scripture is,
even after the fall into sin, a story of *constant achievements*, which,
although always called into question and threatened by sin, are
nonetheless repeated, increased and extended in response to the
divine vocation given from the beginning to man and to woman
(cf. Gen 1:26-28) and inscribed in the image which they received.

It is logical to conclude, at least on the part of those who
believe in the word of God, that today's "development" is to be
seen as a moment in the story which began at creation, a story

which is constantly endangered by reason of infidelity to the Creator's will, and especially by the temptation to idolatry. But this "development" fundamentally corresponds to the first premises. Anyone wishing to renounce the *difficult yet noble task* of improving the lot of man in his totality, and of all people, with the excuse that the struggle is difficult and that constant effort is required, or simply because of the experience of defeat and the need to begin again, that person would be betraying the will of God the Creator. In this regard, in the Encyclical *Laborem Exercens* I referred to man's vocation to work, in order to emphasize the idea that it is always man who is the protagonist of development.[54]

Indeed, the Lord Jesus himself, in the parable of the talents, emphasizes the severe treatment given to the man who dared to hide the gift received: "You wicked and slothful servant! You knew that I reap where I have not sowed and gather where I have not winnowed? . . . So take the talent from him, and give it to him who has the ten talents" (Mt 25:26-28). It falls to us, who receive the gifts of God in order to make them fruitful, to "sow" and "reap." If we do not, even what we have will be taken away from us.

A deeper study of these harsh words will make us commit ourselves more resolutely to the *duty*, which is urgent for everyone today, to work together for the full development of others: "development of the whole human being and of all people."[55]

31. *Faith in Christ the Redeemer,* while it illuminates from within the nature of development, also guides us in the task of collaboration. In the Letter of St. Paul to the Colossians, we read that Christ is "the first-born of all creation," and that "all things were created through him" and for him (1:15-16). In fact, "all things hold together in him," since "in him all the fullness of God was pleased to dwell, and through him to reconcile to himself all things" (v. 20).

A part of this divine plan, which begins from eternity in Christ, the perfect "image" of the Father, and which culminates

---

54. Cf. Encyclical *Laborem Exercens* (September 14, 1981), n. 4: *AAS* 73 (1981), pp. 584f.; Paul VI, Encyclical *Populorum Progressio*, n. 15: *loc. cit.*, p. 265.

55. Encyclical *Populorum Progressio*, n. 42: *loc. cit.*, p. 278.

in him, "the firstborn from the dead" (v. 18), *is our own history*,
marked by our personal and collective effort to raise up the
human condition and to overcome the obstacles which are con-
tinually arising along our way. It thus prepares us to share in the
fullness which "dwells in the Lord" and which he communi-
cates "to his body, which is the Church" (v. 18; cf. Eph 1:22-23).
At the same time sin, which is always attempting to trap us and
which jeopardizes our human achievements, is conquered and
redeemed by the "reconciliation" accomplished by Christ (cf.
Col 1:20).

Here the perspectives widen. The dream of "unlimited progress" reappears, radically transformed by the *new outlook* created
by Christian faith, assuring us that progress is possible only because God the Father has decided from the beginning to make
man a sharer of his glory in Jesus Christ risen from the dead, in
whom "we have redemption through his blood . . . the forgiveness of our trespasses" (Eph 1:7). In him God wished to conquer
sin and make it serve our greater good,[56] which infinitely surpasses what progress could achieve.

We can say therefore—as we struggle amidst the obscurities
and deficiencies of *underdevelopment* and *superdevelopment*—
that one day this corruptible body will put on incorruptibility,
this mortal body immortality (cf. 1 Cor 15:54), when the Lord
"delivers the Kingdom to God the Father" (v. 24) and all the
works and actions that are worthy of man will be redeemed.

Furthermore, the concept of faith makes quite clear the reasons which impel the *Church* to concern herself with the problems of development, to consider them a *duty of her pastoral ministry*, and to urge all to think about the nature and characteristics
of authentic human development. Through her commitment
she desires, on the one hand, to place herself at the service of the
divine plan which is meant to order all things to the fullness
which dwells in Christ (cf. Col 1:19) and which he communicated to his body; and on the other hand she desires to respond
to her fundamental vocation of being a "sacrament," that is to

---

56. Cf. *Praeconium Paschale, Missale Romanum*, ed. typ. altera, 1975,
p. 272: "O certe necessarium Adae peccatum, quod Christi morte deletum
est! O felix culpa, quae talem ac tantum meruit habere Redemptorem!"

say "a sign and instrument of intimate union with God and of the unity of the whole human race."[57]

Some Fathers of the Church were inspired by this idea to develop in original ways a concept of the *meaning of history* and of *human work*, directed towards a goal which surpasses this meaning and which is always defined by its relationship to the work of Christ. In other words, one can find in the teaching of the Fathers an *optimistic vision* of history and work, that is to say of the *perennial value* of authentic human achievements, inasmuch as they are redeemed by Christ and destined for the promised Kingdom.[58]

Thus, part of the *teaching* and most ancient *practice* of the Church is her conviction that she is obliged by her vocation— she herself, her ministers and each of her members—to relieve the misery of the suffering, both far and near, not only out of her "abundance" but also out of her "necessities." Faced by cases of need, one cannot ignore them in favor of superfluous church ornaments and costly furnishings for divine worship; on the contrary it could be obligatory to sell these goods in order to provide food, drink, clothing and shelter for those who lack these things.[59] As has been already noted, here we are shown a *"hierarchy of values"*—in the framework of the right to property—between "having" and "being," especially when the "having" of a few can be to the detriment of the "being" of many others.

In his Encyclical Pope Paul VI stands in the line of this teaching, taking his inspiration from the Pastoral Constitution *Gaudium et Spes*.[60] For my own part, I wish to insist once more

57. Second Vatican Ecumenical Council, Dogmatic Constitution on the Church, *Lumen Gentium*, n. 1.

58. Cf., for example, St. Basil the Great, *Regulae Fusius Tractatae, Interrogatio* XXXVII, nn. 1-2: PG 31, 1009-1012; Theodoret of Cyr., *De Providentia, Oratio* VII: PG 83, 665-686; St. Augustine, *De Civitate Dei*, XIX, n. 17: CCL 48, 683-685.

59. Cf., for example, St. John Chrysostom, *In Evang. S. Matthaei, Hom.* 50, 3-4: PG 58, 508-510; St. Ambrose, *De Officiis Ministrorum*, lib. II, XXVIII, 136-140: PL 16, 139-141; St. Possidius, *Vita S. Augustini Episcopi*, XXIV: PL 32, 53f.

60. Encyclical *Populorum Progressio*, n. 23: *loc. cit.*, p. 268: "'If someone who has the riches of this world sees his brother in need and closes his heart to him, how does the love of God abide in him?' (1 Jn 3:17). It is well known how strong were the words used by the Fathers of the Church to

on the seriousness and urgency of that teaching, and I ask the Lord to give all Christians the strength to put it faithfully into practice.

32. The obligation to commit oneself to the development of peoples is not just an *individual* duty, and still less an *individualistic* one, as if it were possible to achieve this development through the isolated efforts of each individual. It is an imperative which obliges *each and every* man and woman, as well as societies and nations. In particular, it obliges the Catholic Church and the other Churches and Ecclesial Communities, with which we are completely willing to collaborate in this field. In this sense, just as we Catholics invite our Christian brethren to share in our initiatives, so too we declare that we are ready to collaborate in theirs, and we welcome the invitations presented to us. In this pursuit of integral human development we can also do much with the members of other religions, as in fact is being done in various places.

Collaboration in the development of the whole person and of every human being is in fact a duty *of all towards all*, and must be shared by the four parts of the world: East and West, North and South; or, as we say today, by the different "worlds." If, on the contrary, people try to achieve it in only one part, or in only one world, they do so at the expense of the others; and, precisely because the others are ignored, their own development becomes exaggerated and misdirected.

Peoples or *nations* too have a right to their own full development, which while including—as already said—the economic and social aspects, should also include individual cultural identity and openness to the transcendent. Not even the need for development can be used as an excuse for imposing on others one's own way of life or own religious belief.

33. Nor would a type of development which did not respect and promote *human rights*—personal and social, economic and political, including the *rights of nations and of peoples*—be really *worthy of man*.

---

describe the proper attitude of persons who possess anything toward persons in need." In the previous number, the Pope had cited n. 69 of the Pastoral Constitution, *Gaudium et Spes*, of the Second Vatican Ecumenical Council.

Today, perhaps more than in the past, the *intrinsic contradiction* of a development limited *only* to its economic element is seen more clearly. Such development easily subjects the human person and his deepest needs to the demands of economic planning and selfish profit.

The *intrinsic connection* between authentic development and respect for human rights once again reveals the *moral* character of development: the true elevation of man, in conformity with the natural and historical vocation of each individual, is not attained *only* by exploiting the abundance of goods and services, or by having available perfect infrastructures.

When individuals and communities do not see a rigorous respect for the moral, cultural and spiritual requirements, based on the dignity of the person and on the proper identity of each community, beginning with the family and religious societies, then all the rest—availability of goods, abundance of technical resources applied to daily life, a certain level of material well-being—will prove unsatisfying and in the end contemptible. The Lord clearly says this in the Gospel, when he calls the attention of all to the true hierarchy of values: "For what will it profit a man, if he gains the whole world and forfeits his life?" (Mt 16:26)

True development, in keeping with the *specific* needs of the human being—man or woman, child, adult or old person—implies, especially for those who actively share in this process and are responsible for it, a lively *awareness* of the *value* of the rights of all and of each person. It likewise implies a lively awareness of the need to respect the right of every individual to the full use of the benefits offered by science and technology.

On the *internal level* of every nation, respect for all rights takes on great importance, especially: the right to life at every stage of its existence; the rights of the family, as the basic social community, or "cell of society"; justice in employment relationships; the rights inherent in the life of the political community as such; the rights based on the *transcendent vocation* of the human being, beginning with the right of freedom to profess and practice one's own religious belief.

On the *international level*, that is, the level of relations between States or, in present-day usage, between the different "worlds," there must be complete *respect* for the identity of each people, with its own historical and cultural characteristics. It is likewise essential, as the Encyclical *Populorum Progressio* already asked, to recognize each people's equal right "to be seated at the table of the common banquet,"[61] instead of lying outside the door like Lazarus, while "the dogs come and lick his sores" (cf. Lk 16:21). Both peoples and individuals must enjoy the *fundamental equality*[62] which is the basis, for example, of the Charter of the United Nations Organization: the equality which is the basis of the right of all to share in the process of full development.

In order to be genuine, development must be achieved within the framework of *solidarity* and *freedom*, without ever sacrificing either of them under whatever pretext. The moral character of development and its necessary promotion are emphasized when the most rigorous respect is given to all the demands deriving from the order of *truth* and *good* proper to the human person. Furthermore the Christian who is taught to see that man is the image of God, called to share in the truth and the good which is *God himself*, does not understand a commitment to development and its application which excludes regard and respect for the unique dignity of this "image." In other words, true development must be based on the *love of God and neighbor*, and must help to promote the relationships between individuals and society. This is the "civilization of love" of which Paul VI often spoke.

34. Nor can the moral character of development exclude respect *for the beings which constitute* the natural world, which the ancient Greeks—alluding precisely to the *order* which distinguishes it—called the "cosmos." Such realities also demand respect, by virtue of a threefold consideration which it is useful to reflect upon carefully.

---

61. Cf. Encyclical *Populorum Progressio*, n. 47: ". . . a world where freedom is not an empty word and where the poor man Lazarus can sit down at the same table with the rich man."

62. Cf. *ibid.*, n. 47: "It is a question, rather, of building a world where every man, no matter what his race, religion or nationality, can live a fully human life, freed from servitude imposed on him by other men . . ."; cf. also Second Vatican Ecumenical Council, Pastoral Constitution on the Church in the Modern World, *Gaudium et Spes*, n. 29. Such *fundamental equality* is one of the basic reasons why the Church has always been opposed to every form of racism.

The *first* consideration is the appropriateness of acquiring a *growing awareness* of the fact that one cannot use with impunity the different categories of beings, whether living or inanimate—animals, plants, the natural elements—simply as one wishes, according to one's own economic needs. On the contrary, one must take into account *the nature of each being* and of its *mutual connection* in an ordered system, which is precisely the "cosmos."

The *second consideration* is based on the realization—which is perhaps more urgent—that *natural resources* are limited; some are not, as it is said, *renewable*. Using them as if they were inexhaustible, with *absolute dominion*, seriously endangers their availability not only for the present generation but above all for generations to come.

The *third consideration* refers directly to the consequences of a certain type of development on the *quality of life* in the industrialized zones. We all know that the direct or indirect result of industrialization is, ever more frequently, the pollution of the environment, with serious consequences for the health of the population.

Once again it is evident that development, the planning which governs it, and the way in which resources are used must include respect for moral demands. One of the latter undoubtedly imposes limits on the use of the natural world. The dominion granted to man by the Creator is not an absolute power, nor can one speak of a freedom to "use and misuse," or to dispose of things as one pleases. The limitation imposed from the beginning by the Creator himself and expressed symbolically by the prohibition not to "eat of the fruit of the tree" (cf. Gen 2:16-17) shows clearly enough that, when it comes to the natural world, we are subject not only to biological laws but also to moral ones, which cannot be violated with impunity.

A true concept of development cannot ignore the use of the elements of nature, the renewability of resources and the consequences of haphazard industrialization—three considerations which alert our consciences to the *moral dimension* of development.[63]

---

63. Cf. Homily at Val Visdende (July 12, 1987), n. 5: *L'Osservatore Romano*, July 13-14, 1987; Paul VI, Apostolic Letter *Octogesima Adveniens* (May 14, 1971), n. 21: *AAS* 63 (1971), pp. 416f.

V. A Theological Reading of Modern Problems

35. Precisely because of the essentially moral character of development, it is clear that the *obstacles* to development likewise have a moral character. If in the years since the publication of Pope Paul's Encyclical there has been no development—or very little, irregular, or even contradictory development—the reasons are not only economic. As has already been said, political motives also enter in. For the decisions which either accelerate or slow down the development of peoples are really political in character. In order to overcome the misguided mechanisms mentioned earlier and to replace them with new ones which will be more just and in conformity with the common good of humanity, an effective political will is needed. Unfortunately, after analyzing the situation we have to conclude that this political will has been insufficient.

In a document of a pastoral nature such as this, an analysis limited exclusively to the economic and political causes of underdevelopment (and, *mutatis mutandis*, of so-called superdevelopment) would be incomplete. It is therefore necessary to single out the *moral causes* which, with respect to the behavior of *individuals* considered as *responsible persons*, interfere in such a way as to slow down the course of development and hinder its full achievement.

Similarly, when the scientific and technical resources are available which, with the necessary concrete political decisions, ought to help lead peoples to true development, the main obstacles to development will be overcome only by means of *essentially moral decisions*. For believers, and especially for Christians, these decisions will take their inspiration from the principles of faith, with the help of divine grace.

36. It is important to note therefore that a world which is divided into blocs, sustained by rigid ideologies, and in which instead of interdependence and solidarity different forms of imperialism hold sway, can only be a world subject to structures of sin. The sum total of the negative factors working against a true awareness of the universal *common good*, and the need to further it, gives the impression of creating, in persons and institutions, an obstacle which is difficult to overcome.[64]

If the present situation can be attributed to difficulties of various kinds, it is not out of place to speak of "structures of sin," which, as I stated in my Apostolic Exhortation *Reconciliatio et Paenitentia*, are rooted in personal sin, and thus always linked to the *concrete acts* of individuals who introduce these structures, consolidate them and make them difficult to remove.[65] And thus they grow stronger, spread, and become the source of other sins, and so influence people's behavior.

"Sin" and "structures of sin" are categories which are seldom applied to the situation of the contemporary world. However, one cannot easily gain a profound understanding of the reality that confronts us unless we give a name to the root of the evils which afflict us.

---

64. Cf. Second Vatican Ecumenical Council, Pastoral Constitution on the Church in the Modern World, *Gaudium et Spes*, n. 25.

65. Apostolic Exhortation *Reconciliatio et Paenitentia* (December 2, 1984), n. 16: "Whenever the Church speaks of *situations* of sin, or when she condemns as *social sins* certain situations or the collective behavior of certain social groups, big or small, or even of whole nations and blocs of nations, she knows and she proclaims that such cases of *social sin* are the result of the accumulation and concentration of many *personal sins*. It is a case of the very personal sins of those who cause or support evil or who exploit it; of those who are in a position to avoid, eliminate or at least limit certain social evils but who fail to do so out of laziness, fear or the conspiracy of silence, through secret complicity or indifference; of those who take refuge in the supposed impossibility of changing the world, and also of those who sidestep the effort and sacrifice required, producing specious reasons of a higher order. The real responsibility, then, lies with individuals. A situation—or likewise an institution, a structure, society itself—is not in itself the subject of moral acts. Hence a situation cannot in itself be good or bad": *AAS* 77 (1985), p. 217.

One can certainly speak of "selfishness" and of "short-sightedness," of "mistaken political calculations" and "imprudent economic decisions." And in each of these evaluations one hears an echo of an ethical and moral nature. Man's condition is such that a more profound analysis of individuals' actions and omissions cannot be achieved without implying, in one way or another, judgments or references of an ethical nature.

This evaluation is in itself *positive*, especially if it is completely consistent and if it is based on faith in God and on his law, which commands what is good and forbids evil.

In this consists the difference between socio-political analysis and formal reference to "sin" and the "structures of sin." According to this latter viewpoint, there enter in the will of the Triune God, his plan for humanity, his justice and his mercy. The God who is *rich in mercy, the Redeemer of man, the Lord and giver of life*, requires from people clear-cut attitudes which express themselves also in actions or omissions toward one's neighbor. We have here a reference to the "second tablet" of the Ten Commandments (cf. Ex 20:12-17; Dt 5:16-21). Not to observe these is to offend God and hurt one's neighbor, and to introduce into the world influences and obstacles which go far beyond the actions and brief life span of an individual. This also involves interference in the process of the development of peoples, the delay or slowness of which must be judged also in this light.

37. This *general analysis*, which is religious in nature, can be supplemented by *a number of particular considerations* to demonstrate that among the actions and attitudes opposed to the will of God, the good of neighbor and the "structures" created by them, two are very typical: on the one hand, the *all-consuming desire for profit*, and on the other, *the thirst for power*, with the intention of imposing one's will upon others. In order to characterize better each of these attitudes, one can add the expression: "at any price." In other words, we are faced with the *absolutizing* of human attitudes with all its possible consequences.

Since these attitudes can exist independently of each other, they can be separated; however in today's world both are *indissolubly united*, with one or the other predominating.

Obviously, not only individuals fall victim to this double attitude of sin; nations and blocs can do so too. And this favors even more the introduction of the "structures of sin" of which I have spoken. If certain forms of modern "imperialism" were considered in the light of these moral criteria, we would see that hidden behind certain decisions, apparently inspired only by economics or politics, are real forms of idolatry: of money, ideology, class, technology.

I have wished to introduce this type of analysis above all in order to point out the true *nature* of the evil which faces us with respect to the development of peoples: it is a question of a *moral evil*, the fruit of *many sins* which lead to "structures of sin." To diagnose the evil in this way is to identify precisely, on the level of human conduct, *the path to be followed* in order *to overcome it*.

38. This path is *long and complex*, and what is more it is constantly threatened because of the intrinsic frailty of human resolutions and achievements, and because of the *mutability* of very unpredictable and external circumstances. Nevertheless, one must have the courage to set out on this path, and, where some steps have been taken or a part of the journey made, the courage to go on to the end.

In the context of these reflections, the decision to set out or to continue the journey involves, above all, a *moral* value which men and women of faith recognize as a demand of God's will, the only true foundation of an absolutely binding ethic.

One would hope that also men and women without an explicit faith would be convinced that the obstacles to integral development are not only economic but rest on *more profound attitudes* which human beings can make into absolute values. Thus one would hope that all those who, to some degree or other, are responsible for ensuring a "more human life" for their fellow human beings, whether or not they are inspired by a religious faith, will become fully aware of the urgent need to *change* the *spiritual attitudes* which define each individual's relationship with self, with neighbor, with even the remotest human communities, and with nature itself; and all of this in view of higher values such as the *common good* or, to quote the felicitous expression of the Encyclical *Populorum Progressio*, the full development "of the whole individual and of all people."[66]

For *Christians*, as for all who recognize the precise theological meaning of the word "sin," a change of behavior or mentality

---

66. Encyclical *Populorum Progressio*, n. 42: *loc. cit.*, p. 278.

or mode of existence is called "conversion," to use the language of the Bible (cf. Mk 13:3, 5; Is 30:15). This conversion specifically entails a relationship to God, to the sin committed, to its consequences and hence to one's neighbor, either an individual or a community. It is God, in "whose hands are the hearts of the powerful"[67] and the hearts of all, who according to his own promise and by the power of his Spirit can transform "hearts of stone" into "hearts of flesh" (cf. Ezek 36:26).

On the path toward the desired conversion, toward the overcoming of the moral obstacles to development, it is already possible to point to the *positive* and *moral value* of the growing awareness of *interdependence* among individuals and nations. The fact that men and women in various parts of the world feel personally affected by the injustices and violations of human rights committed in distant countries, countries which perhaps they will never visit, is a further sign of a reality transformed into *awareness*, thus acquiring a *moral* connotation.

It is above all a question of *interdependence*, sensed as a *system determining* relationships in the contemporary world, in its economic, cultural, political and religious elements, and accepted as a *moral category*. When interdependence becomes recognized in this way, the correlative response as a moral and social attitude, as a "virtue," is *solidarity*. This then is not a feeling of vague compassion or shallow distress at the misfortunes of so many people, both near and far. On the contrary, it is *a firm and persevering determination* to commit oneself to the *common good;* that is to say to the good of all and of each individual, because we are *all* really responsible *for all*. This determination is based on the *solid* conviction that what is hindering full development is that desire for profit and that thirst for power already mentioned. These attitudes and "structures of sin" are only conquered—presupposing the help of divine grace—by a *diametrically opposed attitude:* a commitment to the good of one's neighbor with the readiness, in the gospel sense, to "lose oneself" for the sake of the other instead of exploiting him, and to "serve him" instead of oppressing him for one's own advantage (cf. Mt 10:40-42; 20:25; Mk 10:42-45; Lk 22:25-27).

---

67. Cf. *Liturgia Horarum*, Feria III Hebdomadae III[ae] Temporis per annum, Preces ad Vesperas.

39. The exercise of solidarity *within each society* is valid when its members recognize one another as persons. Those who are more influential, because they have a greater share of goods and common services, should feel *responsible* for the weaker and be ready to share with them all they possess. Those who are weaker, for their part, in the same spirit of *solidarity*, should not adopt a purely *passive* attitude or one that is *destructive* of the social fabric, but, while claiming their legitimate rights, should do what they can for the good of all. The intermediate groups, in their turn, should not selfishly insist on their particular interests, but respect the interests of others.

Positive signs in the contemporary world are the *growing awareness* of the solidarity of the poor among themselves, their *efforts to support one another*, and their *public demonstrations* on the social scene which, without recourse to violence, present their own needs and rights in the face of the inefficiency or corruption of the public authorities. By virtue of her own evangelical duty the Church feels called to take her stand beside the poor, to discern the justice of their requests, and to help satisfy them, without losing sight of the good of groups in the context of the common good.

The same criterion is applied by analogy in international relationships. Interdependence must be transformed into *solidarity*, based upon the principle that the goods of creation *are meant for all*. That which human industry produces through the processing of raw materials, with the contribution of work, must serve equally for the good of all.

Surmounting every type of *imperialism* and determination to preserve their *own hegemony*, the stronger and richer nations must have a sense of moral *responsibility* for the other nations, so that a *real international system* may be established which will rest on the foundation of the *equality* of all peoples and on the necessary respect for their legitimate differences. The economically weaker countries, or those still at subsistence level, must be enabled, with the assistance of other peoples and of the international community, to make a contribution of their own to the common good with their treasures of *humanity* and *culture*, which otherwise would be lost for ever.

Solidarity helps us to see the "other"—whether a *person, people or nation*—not just as some kind of instrument, with a work

capacity and physical strength to be exploited at low cost and
then discarded when no longer useful, but as our "neighbor," a
"helper" (cf. Gen 2:18-20), to be made a sharer, on a par with
ourselves, in the banquet of life to which all are equally invited
by God. Hence the importance of reawakening the *religious
awareness* of individuals and peoples.

Thus the exploitation, oppression and annihilation of others
are excluded. These facts, in the present division of the world
into opposing blocs, combine to produce the *danger of war* and
an excessive preoccupation with personal security, often to the
detriment of the autonomy, freedom of decision, and even the
territorial integrity of the weaker nations situated within the so-
called "areas of influence" or "safety belts."

The "structures of sin" and the sins which they produce are
likewise radically opposed to *peace and development*, for development, in the familiar expression of Pope Paul's encyclical, is
"the new name for peace."[68]

In this way, the solidarity which we propose is the *path to peace
and at the same time to development*. For world peace is inconceivable unless the world's leaders come to recognize that *interdependence* in itself demands the abandonment of the politics of
blocs, the sacrifice of all forms of economic, military or political
imperialism, and the transformation of mutual distrust into *collaboration*. This is precisely the *act proper* to solidarity among individuals and nations.

The motto of the pontificate of my esteemed predecessor
Pius XII was *Opus iustitiae pax*, peace as the fruit of justice. Today
one could say, with the same exactness and the same power of
biblical inspiration (cf. Is 32:17; Jas 3:18): *Opus solidaritatis pax*,
peace as the fruit of solidarity.

The goal of peace, so desired by everyone, will certainly be
achieved through the putting into effect of social and international justice, but also through the practice of the virtues
which favor togetherness, and which teach us to live in unity, so
as to build in unity, by giving and receiving, a new society and
a better world.

40. *Solidarity* is undoubtedly a *Christian virtue*. In what has
been said so far it has been possible to identify many points of

---

68. Encyclical *Populorum Progressio*, n. 87: *loc. cit.*, p. 299.

contact between solidarity and *charity*, which is the distinguishing mark of Christ's disciples (cf. Jn 13:35).

In the light of faith, solidarity seeks to go beyond itself, to take on the *specifically Christian* dimension of total gratuity, forgiveness and reconciliation. One's neighbor is then not only a human being with his or her own rights and a fundamental equality with everyone else, but becomes the *living image* of God the Father, redeemed by the blood of Jesus Christ and placed under the permanent action of the Holy Spirit. One's neighbor must therefore be loved, even if an enemy, with the same love with which the Lord loves him or her; and for that person's sake one must be ready for sacrifice, even the ultimate one: to lay down one's life for the brethren (cf. 1 Jn 3:16).

At that point, awareness of the common fatherhood of God, of the brotherhood of all in Christ—"children in the Son"—and of the presence and life-giving action of the Holy Spirit will bring to our vision of the world *a new criterion* for interpreting it. Beyond human and natural bonds, already so close and strong, there is discerned in the light of faith a new *model* of the *unity* of the human race, which must ultimately inspire our *solidarity*. This supreme *model of unity*, which is a reflection of the intimate life of God, one God in three Persons, is what we Christians mean by the word "communion." This specifically Christian communion, jealously preserved, extended and enriched with the Lord's help, is the *soul* of the Church's vocation to be a "sacrament," in the sense already indicated.

Solidarity therefore must play its part in the realization of this divine plan, both on the level of individuals and on the level of national and international society. The "evil mechanisms" and "structures of sin" of which we have spoken can be overcome only through the exercise of the human and Christian solidarity to which the Church calls us and which she tirelessly promotes. Only in this way can such positive energies be fully released for the benefit of development and peace.

Many of the Church's canonized saints offer a *wonderful witness* of such solidarity and can serve as examples in the present difficult circumstances. Among them I wish to recall St. Peter Claver and his service to the slaves at Cartagena de Indias, and St. Maximilian Maria Kolbe, who offered his life in place of a prisoner unknown to him in the concentration camp at Auschwitz.

VI. Some Particular Guidelines

41. The Church does not have *technical solutions* to offer for the problem of underdevelopment as such, as Pope Paul VI already affirmed in his Encyclical.[69] For the Church does not propose economic and political systems or programs, nor does she show preference for one or the other, provided that human dignity is properly respected and promoted, and provided she herself is allowed the room she needs to exercise her ministry in the world.

But the Church is an "expert in humanity,"[70] and this leads her necessarily to extend her religious mission to the various fields in which men and women expend their efforts in search of the always relative happiness which is possible in this world, in line with their dignity as persons.

Following the examples of my predecessors, I must repeat that whatever affects the dignity of individuals and peoples, such as authentic development, cannot be reduced to a "technical" problem. If reduced in this way, development would be emptied of its true content, and this would be an act of *betrayal* of the individuals and peoples whom development is meant to serve.

This is why the Church has *something to say* today, just as twenty years ago, and also in the future, about the nature, conditions, requirements and aims of authentic development, and also about the obstacles which stand in its way. In doing so the Church fulfills her mission to *evangelize*, for she offers her *first*

---

69. Cf. Encyclical *Populorum Progressio*, n. 13: *loc. cit.*, pp. 263f., 296f.
70. Cf. *ibid.*, n. 13: *loc. cit.*, p. 263.

contribution to the solution of the urgent problem of development when she proclaims the truth about Christ, about herself
and about man, applying this truth to a concrete situation.[71]

As her *instrument* for reaching this goal, the Church uses her
social doctrine. In today's difficult situation, a *more exact awareness and a wider diffusion* of the "set of principles for reflection,
criteria for judgment and directives for action" proposed by the
Church's teaching[72] would be of great help in promoting both
the correct definition of the problems being faced and the best
solution to them.

It will thus be seen at once that the questions facing us are
above all moral questions; and that neither the analysis of the
problem of development as such nor the means to overcome the
present difficulties can ignore this essential dimension.

The Church's social doctrine *is not* a "third way" between *liberal capitalism* and *Marxist collectivism*, nor even a possible alternative to other solutions less radically opposed to one another:
rather, it constitutes a *category of its own*. Nor is it an *ideology*, but
rather the *accurate formulation* of the results of a careful reflection on the complex realities of human existence, in society and
in the international order, in the light of faith and of the church's
tradition. Its main aim is to *interpret* these realities, determining
their conformity with or divergence from the lines of the Gospel
teaching on man and his vocation, a vocation which is at once
earthly and transcendent; its aim is thus *to guide* Christian behavior. It therefore belongs to the field, not of *ideology*, but of *theology* and particularly of moral theology.

The teaching and spreading of her social doctrine are part of
the Church's evangelizing mission. And since it is a doctrine
aimed at guiding *people's behavior*, it consequently gives rise to a
"commitment to justice," according to each individual's role,
vocation and circumstances.

The *condemnation* of evils and injustices is also part of that

---

71. Cf. Address at the Opening of the Third General Conference of the
Latin American Bishops (January 28, 1979): *AAS* 71 (1979), pp. 189-196.

72. Congregation for the Doctrine of the Faith, Instruction on Christian
Freedom and Liberation, *Libertatis Conscientia* (March 22, 1986), n. 72: *AAS*
79 (1987), p. 586; Paul VI, Apostolic Letter *Octogesima Adveniens* (May 14,
1971), n. 4: *AAS* 63 (1971), pp. 403f.

ministry of evangelization in the social field which is an aspect of the Church's *prophetic role*. But it should be made clear that *proclamation* is always more important than *condemnation*, and the latter cannot ignore the former, which gives it true solidity and the force of higher motivation.

42. Today more than in the past, the Church's social doctrine must be open to an *international outlook*, in line with the Second Vatican Council,[73] the most recent Encyclicals,[74] and particularly in line with the encyclical which we are commemorating.[75] It will not be superfluous therefore to reexamine and further clarify in this light the characteristic themes and guidelines dealt with by the Magisterium in recent years.

Here I would like to indicate one of them: the *option* or *love of preference* for the poor. This is an option, or a *special form* of primacy in the exercise of Christian charity, to which the whole tradition of the Church bears witness. It affects the life of each Christian inasmuch as he or she seeks to imitate the life of Christ, but it applies equally to our *social responsibilities* and hence to our manner of living, and to the logical decisions to be made concerning the ownership and use of goods.

Today, furthermore, given the worldwide dimension which the social question has assumed,[76] this love of preference for the poor, and the decisions which it inspires in us, cannot but embrace the immense multitudes of the hungry, the needy, the homeless, those without medical care and, above all, those without hope of a better future. It is impossible not to take account of the existence of these realities. To ignore them would mean becoming like the "rich man" who pretended not to know the beggar Lazarus lying at his gate (cf. Lk 16:19-31).[77]

---

73. Cf. Pastoral Constitution on the Church in the Modern World, *Gaudium et Spes*, Part II, Ch. V, Section 2: "Building Up the International Community," nn. 83-90.

74. Cf. John XXIII, Encyclical *Mater et Magistra* (May 15, 1961): *AAS* 53 (1961), p. 440; Encyclical *Pacem in Terris* (April 11, 1963), Part IV: *AAS* 55 (1963), pp. 291-296; Paul VI, Apostolic Letter *Octogesima Adveniens* (May 14, 1971), nn. 2-4: *AAS* 63 (1971), pp. 402-404.

75. Cf. Encyclical *Populorum Progressio*, nn. 3, 9: *loc. cit.*, pp. 258, 261.

76. *Ibid.*, n. 3: *loc. cit.*, p. 258.

77. Encyclical *Populorum Progressio*, n. 47: *loc. cit.*, p. 280; Congregation for the Doctrine of the Faith, Instruction on Christian Freedom and Lib-

Our *daily life* as well as our decisions in the political and economic fields must be marked by these realities. Likewise the *leaders* of nations and the heads of *international bodies*, while they are obliged always to keep in mind the true human dimension as a priority in their development plans, should not forget to give precedence to the phenomenon of growing poverty. Unfortunately, instead of becoming fewer the poor are becoming more numerous, not only in less developed countries but—and this seems no less scandalous—in the more developed ones too.

It is necessary to state once more the characteristic principle of Christian social doctrine: the goods of this world are *originally meant for all*.[78] The right to private property is *valid and necessary*, but it does not nullify the value of this principle. Private property, in fact, is under a "social mortgage,"[79] which means that it has an intrinsically social function, based upon and justified precisely by the principle of the universal destination of goods. Likewise, in this concern for the poor, one must not overlook that *special form of poverty* which consists in being deprived of fundamental human rights, in particular the right to religious freedom and also the right to freedom of economic initiative.

43. The motivating concern for the poor—who are, in the very meaningful term, "the Lord's poor"[80]—must be translated at all levels into concrete actions, until it decisively attains a series of necessary reforms. Each local situation will show what reforms are most urgent and how they can be achieved. But those

---

eration, *Libertatis Conscientia* (March 22, 1986), n. 68: *AAS* 79 (1987), pp. 583f.

78. Cf. Second Vatican Ecumenical Council, Pastoral Constitution on the Church in the Modern World, *Gaudium et Spes*, n. 69; Paul VI, Encyclical *Populorum Progressio*, n. 22: *loc. cit.*, p. 268; Congregation for the Doctrine of the Faith, Instruction on Christian Freedom and Liberation, *Libertatis Conscientia* (March 22, 1986), n. 90: *AAS* 79 (1987), p. 594; St. Thomas Aquinas, *Summa Theol.* II^a II^{ae}, q. 66, art. 2.

79. Cf. Address at the Opening of the Third General Conference of the Latin American Bishops (January 28, 1979): *AAS* 71 (1979), pp. 189-196; *Ad Limina* Address to a group of Polish Bishops (December 17, 1987), n. 6: *L'Osservatore Romano*, December 18, 1987.

80. Because the Lord wished to identify himself with them (Mt 25:31-46) and takes special care of them (cf. Ps 12[11]:6; Lk 1:52f.).

demanded by the situation of international imbalance, as already described, must not be forgotten.

In this respect I wish to mention specifically: the *reform of the international trade system*, which is mortgaged to protectionism and increasing bilateralism; the *reform of the world monetary and financial system*, today recognized as inadequate; the *question of technological exchanges* and their proper use; the *need* for a *review of the structure of the existing international organizations*, in the framework of an international juridical order.

The *international trade system* today frequently discriminates against the products of the young industries of the developing countries and discourages the producers of raw materials. There exists, too, a kind of *international division of labor*, whereby the low-cost products of certain countries which lack effective labor laws or which are too weak to apply them are sold in other parts of the world at considerable profit for the companies engaged in this form of production, which knows no frontiers.

The *world monetary and financial system* is marked by an excessive fluctuation of exchange rates and interest rates, to the detriment of the balance of payments and the debt situation of the poorer countries.

Forms of technology and their transfer constitute today one of the major problems of international exchange and of the grave damage deriving therefrom. There are quite frequent cases of developing countries being denied needed forms of technology or sent useless ones.

In the opinion of many, the *international organizations* seem to be at a stage of their existence when their operating methods, operating costs and effectiveness need careful review and possible correction. Obviously, such a delicate process cannot be put into effect without the collaboration of all. This presupposes the overcoming of political rivalries and the renouncing of all desire to manipulate these organizations, which exist solely for *the common good*.

The existing institutions and organizations have worked well for the benefit of peoples. Nevertheless, humanity today is in a new and more difficult phase of its genuine development. It needs a *greater degree of international ordering*, at the service of the societies, economies and cultures of the whole world.

44. Development demands above all a spirit of initiative on

the part of the countries which need it.[81] Each of them must act in accordance with its own responsibilities, *not expecting everything* from the more favored countries, and acting in collaboration with others in the same situation. Each must discover and use to the best advantage its *own area of freedom*. Each must make itself capable of initiatives responding to its own needs as a society. Each must likewise realize its true needs, as well as the rights and duties which oblige it to respond to them. The development of peoples begins and is most appropriately accomplished in the dedication of each people to its own development, in collaboration with others.

It is important then that as far as possible *the developing nations themselves* should favor the *self-affirmation* of each citizen, through access to a wider culture and a free flow of information. Whatever promotes *literacy* and the *basic education* which completes and deepens it is a direct contribution to true development, as the encyclical *Populorum Progressio* proposed.[82] These goals are still far from being reached in so many parts of the world.

In order to take this path, *the nations themselves* will have to identify their own *priorities* and clearly recognize their own needs, according to the particular conditions of their people, their geographical setting and their cultural traditions.

Some nations will have to increase *food production*, in order to have always available what is needed for subsistence and daily life. In the modern world—where starvation claims so many victims, especially among the very young—there are examples of not particularly developed nations which have nevertheless achieved the goal of *food self-sufficiency* and have even become food exporters.

Other nations need to reform certain unjust structures, and in particular their *political institutions*, in order to replace cor-

---

81. Encyclical *Populorum Progressio*, n. 55: *loc. cit.*, p. 284: "These are the men and women that need to be helped, that need to be convinced to take into their own hands their development, gradually acquiring the means"; cf. Pastoral Constitution on the Church in the Modern World, *Gaudium et Spes*, n. 86.

82. Encyclical *Populorum Progressio*, n. 35: *loc. cit.*, p. 274: "Basic education is the first objective of a plan of development."

rupt, dictatorial and authoritarian forms of government by *democratic* and *participatory* ones. This is a process which we hope will spread and grow stronger. For the "health" of a political community—as expressed in the free and responsible participation of all citizens in public affairs, in the rule of the law and in respect for the promotion of human rights—is the *necessary condition and sure guarantee* of the development of "the whole individual and of all people."

45. None of what has been said can be achieved *without the collaboration of all*—especially the international community—in the framework of a *solidarity* which includes everyone, beginning with the most neglected. But the developing nations themselves have the duty to practice *solidarity among themselves* and with the neediest countries of the world.

It is desirable, for example, that nations of the *same geographical area* should establish *forms of cooperation* which will make them less dependent on more powerful producers; they should open their frontiers to the products of the area; they should examine how their products might complement one another; they should combine in order to set up those services which each one separately is incapable of providing; they should extend cooperation to the monetary and financial sector.

Interdependence is already a reality in many of these countries. To acknowledge it, in such a way as to make it more operative, represents an alternative to excessive dependence on richer and more powerful nations, as part of the hoped-for development, without opposing anyone, but discovering and making best use of the country's *own potential*. The developing countries belonging to one geographical area, especially those included in the term "South," can and ought to set up *new regional organizations* inspired by criteria of *equality, freedom and participation* in the comity of nations—as is already happening with promising results.

An essential condition for global *solidarity* is autonomy and free self-determination, also within associations such as those indicated. But at the same time solidarity demands a readiness to accept the sacrifices necessary for the good of the whole world community.

VII. Conclusion

46. Peoples and individuals aspire to be free: their search for full development signals their desire to overcome the many obstacles preventing them from enjoying a "more human life."

Recently, in the period following the publication of the encyclical *Populorum Progressio,* a new way of confronting the problems of poverty and underdevelopment has spread in some areas of the world, especially in Latin America. This approach makes *liberation* the fundamental category and the first principle of action. The positive values, as well as the deviations and risks of deviation, which are damaging to the faith and are connected with this form of theological reflection and method, have been appropriately pointed out by the Church's Magisterium.[83]

It is fitting to add that the aspiration to freedom from all forms of slavery affecting the individual and society is something *noble* and *legitimate.* This in fact is the purpose of development, or rather liberation and development, taking into account the intimate connection between the two.

Development which is merely economic is incapable of setting man free; on the contrary, it will end by enslaving him further. Development that does not include the *cultural, transcendent and religious dimensions* of man and society, to the extent that

---

83. Cf. Congregation for the Doctrine of the Faith, Instruction on Certain Aspects of the "Theology of Liberation," *Libertatis Nuntius* (August 6, 1984), Introduction: *AAS* 76 (1984), pp. 876f.

it does not recognize the existence of such dimensions and does not endeavor to direct its goals and priorities toward the same, is *even less* conducive to authentic liberation. Human beings are totally free only when they are completely *themselves*, in the fullness of their rights and duties. The same can be said about society as a whole.

The principal obstacle to be overcome on the way to authentic liberation is *sin* and the *structures* produced by sin as it multiplies and spreads.[84]

The freedom with which Christ has set us free (cf. Gal 5:1) encourages us to become the *servants* of all. Thus the process of *development* and *liberation* takes concrete shape in the exercise of *solidarity*, that is to say in the love and service of neighbor, especially of the poorest: "For where truth and love are missing, the process of liberation results in the death of a freedom which will have lost all support."[85]

47. In the context of the *sad experiences* of recent years and of the *mainly negative picture* of the present moment, the Church must strongly affirm the *possibility* of overcoming the obstacles which, by excess or by defect, stand in the way of development. And she must affirm her confidence in a *true liberation*. Ultimately, this confidence and this possibility are based on the *Church's awareness* of the divine promise guaranteeing that our present history does not remain closed in upon itself but is open to the Kingdom of God.

The Church has *confidence also in man*, though she knows the evil of which he is capable. For she well knows that—in spite of the heritage of sin, and the sin which each one is capable of committing—there exist in the human person sufficient qualities and energies, a fundamental "goodness" (cf. Gen 1:31), because he is the image of the Creator, placed under the redemptive influence of Christ, who "united himself in some fashion with

---

84. Cf. Apostolic Exhortation *Reconciliatio et Paenitentia* (December 2, 1984), n. 16: *AAS* 77 (1985), pp. 213-217; Congregation for the Doctrine of the Faith, Instruction on Christian Freedom and Liberation, *Libertatis Conscientia* (March 22, 1986, nn. 38, 42: *AAS* 79 (1987), pp. 569, 571.

85. Congregation for the Doctrine of the Faith, Instruction on Christian Freedom and Liberation, *Libertatis Conscientia* (March 22, 1986), n. 24: *AAS* 79 (1987), p. 564.

every man,"[86] and because the efficacious action of the Holy Spirit "fills the earth" (Wis 1:7).

There is no justification then for despair or pessimism or inertia. Though it be with sorrow, it must be said that just as one may sin through selfishness and the desire for excessive profit and power, *one may also be found wanting* with regard to the urgent needs of multitudes of human beings submerged in conditions of underdevelopment, through *fear, indecision* and, basically, through *cowardice.* We are *all* called, indeed *obliged,* to face the tremendous challenge of the last decade of the second Millennium, also because the present dangers threaten everyone: a world economic crisis, a war without frontiers, without winners or losers. In the face of such a threat, the distinction between rich individuals and countries and poor individuals and countries *will have little value,* except that a greater responsibility rests on those who have more and can do more.

This is not however the *sole motive or even the most important one.* At stake is the *dignity of the human person,* whose *defense* and *promotion* have been entrusted to us by the Creator, and to whom the men and women at every moment of history are strictly and responsibly *in debt.* As many people are already more or less clearly aware, the present situation *does not seem to correspond to* this dignity. *Every individual* is called upon to play his or her part in this *peaceful* campaign, a campaign to be conducted by *peaceful* means, in order to secure *development in peace,* in order to safeguard nature itself and the world about us. The Church too feels profoundly involved in this enterprise, and she hopes for its ultimate success.

Consequently, following the example of Pope Paul VI with his Encyclical *Populorum Progressio,*[87] I wish *to appeal* with simplicity and humility to *everyone,* to all men and women without exception. I wish to ask them to be convinced of the seriousness of the present moment and of each one's individual responsi-

---

86. Cf. Pastoral Constitution on the Church in the Modern World, *Gaudium et Spes,* n. 22; John Paul II, Encyclical *Redemptor Hominis* (March 4, 1979), n. 8: *AAS* 71 (1979), p. 272.

87. Encyclical *Populorum Progressio,* n. 5: *loc. cit.,* p. 259: "We believe that all men of good will, together with our Catholic sons and daughters and our Christian brethren, can and should agree on this program"; cf. also nn. 81-83, 87: *loc. cit.,* pp. 296-298, 299.

bility, and to implement—by the way they live as individuals and as families, by the use of their resources, by their civic activity, by contributing to economic and political decisions and by personal commitment to national and international undertakings—the *measures* inspired by solidarity and love of preference for the poor. This is what is demanded by the present moment and above all by the very dignity of the human person, the indestructible image of God the Creator, which is *identical* in each one of us.

In this commitment, the sons and daughters of the Church must serve as examples and guides, for they are called upon, in conformity with the program announced by Jesus himself in the synagogue at Nazareth, to "preach good news to the poor . . . to proclaim release to the captives and recovering of sight to the blind, to set at liberty those who are oppressed, to proclaim the acceptable year of the Lord" (Lk 4:18-19). It is appropriate to emphasize the *preeminent role* that belongs to the *laity*, both men and women, as was reaffirmed in the recent Assembly of the Synod. It is their task to animate temporal realities with Christian commitment, by which they show that they are witnesses and agents of peace and justice.

I wish to address especially those who, through the sacrament of Baptism and the profession of the same Creed, *share* a *real*, though imperfect, *communion* with us. I am certain that the concern expressed in this Encyclical as well as the motives inspiring it *will be familiar to them*, for these motives are inspired by the Gospel of Jesus Christ. We can find here a new invitation *to bear witness together* to our *common convictions* concerning the dignity of man, created by God, redeemed by Christ, made holy by the Spirit and called upon in this world to live a life in conformity with this dignity.

I likewise address this appeal to the Jewish people, who share with us the inheritance of Abraham, "our father in faith" (cf. Rm 4:11f.)[88] and the tradition of the Old Testament, as well as to the Muslims who, like us, believe in a just and merciful God. And I extend it to all the followers of *the world's great religions*.

The meeting held last October 27 in Assisi, the city of St. Fran-

---

88. Cf. Second Vatican Ecumenical Council, Declaration on the Relationship of the Church to Non-Christian Religions, *Nostra Aetate*, n. 4.

cis, in order to pray for and commit ourselves to *peace*—each one in fidelity to his own religious profession—showed how much peace and, as its necessary condition, the development of the whole person and of all peoples, are also a *matter of religion,* and how the full achievement of both the one and the other depends on our *fidelity* to our vocation as men and women of faith. For it depends, above all, *on God*.

48. The Church well knows that *no temporal achievement* is to be identified with the Kingdom of God, but that all such achievements simply *reflect* and in a sense *anticipate* the glory of the Kingdom, the Kingdom which we await at the end of history, when the Lord will come again. But that expectation can never be an excuse for lack of concern for people in their concrete personal situations and in their social, national and international life, since the former is conditioned by the latter, especially today.

However imperfect and temporary are all the things that can and ought to be done through the combined efforts of everyone and through divine grace, at a given moment of history, in order to make people's lives "more human," nothing will be *lost* or *will have been in vain*. This is the teaching of the Second Vatican Council, in an enlightening passage of the Pastoral Constitution *Gaudium et Spes:* "When we have spread on earth the fruits of our nature and our enterprise—human dignity, fraternal communion, and freedom—according to the command of he Lord and in his Spirit, we will find them once again, cleansed this time from the stain of sin, illumined and transfigured, when Christ presents to his Father an eternal and universal kingdom . . . here on earth that kingdom is already present in mystery."[89]

The Kingdom of God becomes *present* above all in the celebration of the *sacrament of the Eucharist,* which is the Lord's Sacrifice. In that celebration the fruits of the earth and the work of human hands—the bread and wine—are transformed mysteriously, but really and substantially, through the power of the Holy Spirit and the words of the minister, *into the Body and Blood* of the Lord Jesus Christ, the Son of God and Son of Mary, through whom the *Kingdom of the Father* has been made present in our midst.

---

89. *Gaudium et Spes*, n. 39.

The goods of this world and the work of our hands—the bread and wine—serve for the coming of the *definitive Kingdom*, since the Lord, through his Spirit, takes them up into himself in order to offer himself to the Father and to offer us with himself in the renewal of his one Sacrifice, which anticipates God's Kingdom and proclaims its final coming.

Thus the Lord *unites us with himself* through the Eucharist— Sacrament and Sacrifice—and he *unites us with himself and with one another* by a bond stronger than any natural union; and thus united, *he sends us* into the whole world to bear witness, through faith and works, to God's love, preparing the coming of his Kingdom and anticipating it, though in the obscurity of the present time.

All of us who take part in the Eucharist are called to discover, through this sacrament, the profound *meaning* of our actions in the world in favor of development and peace; and to receive from it the strength to commit ourselves ever more generously, following the example of Christ, who in this sacrament lays down his life for his friends (cf. Jn 15:13). Our personal commitment, like Christ's and in union with his, will not be in vain but certainly fruitful.

49. I have called the current *Marian* Year in order that the Catholic faithful may look more and more to Mary, who goes before us on the pilgrimage of faith[90] and with maternal care intercedes for us before her Son, our Redeemer. I wish to *entrust to her* and to *her intercession* this *difficult moment* of the modern world, and the efforts that are being made and will be made, often with great suffering, in order to contribute to the true development of peoples proposed and proclaimed by my predecessor Paul VI.

In keeping with Christian piety through the ages, we present to the Blessed Virgin difficult individual situations, so that she may place them before her Son, asking that he *alleviate and change* them. But we also present to her *social situations* and *the international crisis* itself, in their worrying aspects of poverty, unemployment, shortage of food, the arms race, contempt for human

---

90. Cf. Second Vatican Ecumenical Council, Dogmatic Constitution on the Church, *Lumen Gentium*, n. 58; John Paul II, Encyclical *Redemptoris Mater* (March 25, 1987), nn. 5-6: *AAS* 79 (1987), pp. 365-367.

rights, and situations or dangers of conflict, partial or total. In a filial spirit we wish to place all this before her "eyes of mercy," repeating once more with faith and hope the ancient antiphon: "Holy Mother of God, despise not our petitions in our necessities, but deliver us always from all dangers, O glorious and blessed Virgin."

Mary most holy, our Mother and Queen, is the one who turns to her Son and says: "They have no more wine" (Jn 2:3). She is also the one who praises God the Father, because "he has put down the mighty from their thrones and exalted those of low degree; he has filled the hungry with good things, and the rich he has sent empty away" (Lk 1:52 53). Her maternal concern extends to the *personal* and *social* aspects of people's life on earth.[91]

Before the Most Blessed Trinity, I entrust to Mary all that I have written in this Encyclical, and I invite all to reflect and actively commit themselves to promoting the true development of peoples, as the prayer of the Mass for this intention states so well: "Father, you have given all peoples one common origin, and your will is to gather them as one family in yourself. Fill the hearts of all with the fire of your love, and the desire to ensure justice for all their brothers and sisters. By sharing the good things you give us, may we secure justice and equality for every human being, an end to all division and a human society built on love and peace."[92]

This, in conclusion, is what I ask in the name of all my brothers and sisters, to whom I send a special blessing as a sign of greeting and good wishes.

Given in Rome, at St. Peter's, on December 30 of the year 1987, the tenth of my Pontificate.

---

91. Cf. Paul VI, Apostolic Exhortation *Marialis Cultus* (February 2, 1974), n. 37: *AAS* 66 (1974), pp. 148f.; John Paul II, Homily at the Shrine of Our Lady of Zapopan, Mexico (January 30, 1979), n. 4: *AAS* 71 (1979), p. 230.

92. Collect of the Mass "For the Development of Peoples": *Missale Romanum*, ed. typ. altera, 1975, p. 820.

COMMENTARIES

The Development of Nations

MICHAEL NOVAK

No encyclical of John Paul II's has stirred as much international controversy as "Concern for Social Reality," *Sollicitudo Rei Socialis*. Although the text did not appear until the end of February 1988, it was backdated by fifty-one days so as to be dated in 1987 (30 December), in time to mark at least the year of Paul VI's encyclical, *Populorum Progressio* (26 March 1967). Nearly a year late, Pope John Paul II's encyclical shows clear signs of representing in its drafting several different factions. Yet it also shows many signs both of the pope's vivid experience under Marxist regimes and of his own personal phraseology.

The "creation theology" so brilliantly established in John Paul II's *Laborem Exercens* (15 September 1981) once again supplies the basic architecture of the new letter. This foundation in the dynamic of Genesis firmly places papal social thought in the narrative line of the Anglo-American experiment in political economy. In that tradition modern institutions of economic, political, and cultural development first entered into history.

The American experiment, in particular, springs from, and is inconceivable apart from, two biblical narratives, Creation and Exodus.[1] The design of the American *ordo* cannot be understood apart from a practical acceptance of the Jewish-Christian doctrine that from sinful persons sinful structures come. Any workable *ordo*, therefore, must include checks and balances against

---

1. See Russell Kirk, *The Roots of American Order* (LaSalle, Illinois: Open Court, 1974), chap. 2, "The Law and the Prophets."

man's sinful tendencies. On the seal of the United States the image of a pyramid reminds Americans, who wandered across the desolate ocean from the comforts of Europe to a New Eden, that they had been preceded by the people of Israel, who wandered in the desert from the fleshpots of Egypt toward the Promised Land. Above this symbol is the invocation of the Creator who cares for particulars and singulars: "*Annuit Coeptis:* [Providence] smiled on our beginnings." The new order is designed to be a "system of natural liberty," fitted to the nature of free persons capable of governing themselves through reflection and choice.[2]

"The God Who gave us life," Thomas Jefferson wrote, appealing to Genesis, "gave us liberty."[3] And in the Declaration of Independence of 4 July 1776, the revolutionary Continental Congress announced:

> We hold these truths to be self-evident: that all men are created equal, that they are endowed by their Creator with certain unalienable rights, that among these are life, liberty, and the pursuit of happiness. That to secure these rights, governments are instituted among men, deriving their just powers from the consent of the governed.

George Weigel, whose survey of the long Catholic tradition of political thought, *Tranquillitas Ordinis*, has already established itself as a classic of our time, has elsewhere treated of the strong steps forward Pope John Paul II has taken in *Sollicitudo* concerning the importance of liberal *democratic* institutions to the fulfill-

---

2. The Continental Congress asked Benjamin Franklin, John Adams, and Thomas Jefferson "to prepare a device for a Seal of the United States of North America." Their design included "Pharaoh sitting in an open Chariot, a Crown on his head and a sword in his hand passing through the divided Waters of the Red Sea in pursuit of the Israelites." U.S. Department of State, *The Seal of the United States: How It was Developed and Adopted* (Washington, D.C.: Department of State, 1892), pp. 5-6. See also Richard S. Patterson and Richardson Dougall, *The Eagle and the Shield: A History of the Great Seal of the United States* (Washington, D.C.: U.S. Government Printing Office, 1976); Leonard Wilson, *The Coat of Arms, Crest and Great Seal of the United States of America* (San Diego: by the author, 1928).

3. Thomas Jefferson, "A Summary View of the Rights of British America, 1774," in Adrienne Koch and William Peden, eds., *The Life and Selected Writings of Thomas Jefferson* (New York: Modern Library, 1972), p. 311.

ment of Catholic moral theology.[4] My task in this essay is to analyze the fresh steps *Sollicitudo* has taken in identifying the *economic* institutions necessary to such fulfillment.

Four Classic Principles

The four classic principles of Catholic teaching about the good and realistic society on which *Sollicitudo Rei Socialis* draws can be briefly stated: (1) A good and realistic human society must take account of the role of original sin and of persistent actual sins of commission and omission, which mark every stage of human development until the Second Coming. Because sinful humans cannot create sinless structures, realism precludes dreams of utopia. Every actual human institution is marked by sins that spring from the human heart.

(2) As the root of sin lies in human liberty, so also does the dignity of free men and women. Dignity springs from liberty. It arises from the human capacity for *reflection* and *choice*, a capacity that imprints within every human being the "image of God, the Creator," and endows every person with the unalienable rights inherent in such liberty.[5]

(3) As God the Creator is One, so is the human race one. The human race is social, familial even (one family of the One God). Every person is by vocation committed to advancing the common good of all. The goods of creation are destined for all, and the work of all is necessary to bring creation to fruition.

(4) In order to secure human rights, governments are necessarily formed among humans. They must be rooted in the participation and consent of all the people; the people are sovereign. A corollary of this vision is the "principle of subsid-

---

4. See George Weigel, *Tranquillitas Ordinis: The Present Failure and Future Promise of American Catholic Thought on War and Peace* (New York: Oxford University Press, 1987); and his essay in this volume.

5. In the first paragraph of the *Federalist*, Alexander Hamilton writes: "It seems to have been reserved to the people of this country, by their conduct and example, to decide the important question, whether societies of men are really capable or not of establishing good government from *reflection* and *choice*, or whether they are forever destined to depend for their political constitutions on *accident* and *force*" (italics added).

iarity."[6] Governments are necessary both for securing human
rights (restraining the sinfulness of one human regarding
others) and for achieving the common good through respecting
the dignity of every person. Yet, unable to escape the universal
fact of sin, government is simultaneously both an agent of the
common good and a threat to the common good. Government,
therefore, must be limited. The state is a *subsidium*, a help, and
not an end in itself. To protect the dignity of the person and the
free associations through which the social nature of humans is
normally expressed, the state is expressly forbidden to do those
things that persons and their free associations can do for themselves. It is empowered to come to their assistance (*subsidium*)
only in those matters in which its powers are necessary for the
common good. The state in Catholic teaching is a *limited* state.
It loses legitimacy if it violates the human liberty and dignity it
is formed to serve. Human persons are not made for the state,
but the state for persons.

Each of these fundamental principles of Catholic social teaching is, in fact, embodied in such founding documents of the
United States as the Declaration of Independence, the Constitution, the *Federalist*, and other classics of the American tradition.
Like the American framers, Pope John Paul II—and, in general,
the Catholic natural law tradition favored by modern popes
since Leo XIII—goes back to Genesis and its universalist vision
of all humanity as one. The American framers appealed to no
specifically *American* rights, only to *human* rights belonging to
every human everywhere. That is why they spoke of a New
Order "of the Ages," wrote of the system of *natural* liberty (not

---

6. "It is a fundamental principle of social philosophy, fixed and un-
changeable," Pius XI writes, "that one should not withdraw from individuals and commit to the community what they can accomplish by
their own enterprise and industry. So, too, it is an injustice and at the same
time a grave evil and a disturbance of right order, to transfer to the larger
and higher collectivity functions which can be performed and provided
for by lesser and subordinate bodies. . . .

"The more faithfully this principle of 'subsidiarity' is followed and a
hierarchical order prevails among the various organizations, the more ex-
cellent will be the authority and efficiency of society, and the happier and
more prosperous the condition of the commonwealth" (*Quadragesimo
Anno*, 79-80).

merely of "American" liberty), looked to unalienable rights endowed in humans "by their Creator," and dared to entrust their fate to the care of Providence. Their experiment tested certain propositions for all humankind, not solely for themselves.

Moreover, in appealing to "liberty," the American framers did not mean *any* liberty, such as egoism or licentiousness,[7] but rather—as Pope John Paul II noted in Miami in the autumn of 1987—"ordered liberty."[8] A classic American hymn defines such ordered liberty simply: "Confirm thy soul in self-control/ Thy liberty in law." The Statue of Liberty, gift to America from France's liberal party in 1886, invokes a similar lesson: The Lady holds the light of Reason aloft in one hand, against the darkness, and in the other holds a tablet of the law (marked "MDCCLXXVI" as if to recall "We hold these truths . . .").

Many of the texts in *Sollicitudo Rei Socialis* come closer to expressing this vision—dear in one version to Catholic social teaching, and in another to the classical American tradition—than any prior document of any pope. You will not find such consonance in Leo XIII, Pius XI, or Paul VI. Only in the "Christmas Messages" of Pius XII during the dark days of the struggle against Nazi totalitarianism,[9] and in John XXIII's *Pacem in Ter-*

---

7. In an 1858 report to the Holy See, Archbishop John Hughes explained how Americans understand liberty: "Liberty, in this Country, has a very clear and specific meaning. It is not understood in Europe, as it is here. Here, it means the vindication of personal rights; the fair support of public laws; the maintenance, at all hazards, of public order, according to those laws; the right to change them when they are found to be absurd or oppressive" (John Tracy Ellis, ed., *Documents of American Catholic History* [Milwaukee: Bruce Publishing Co., 1956], pp. 338-39).

8. "From the beginning of America, freedom was directed to forming a well-ordered society and to promoting its peaceful life. Freedom was channeled to the fullness of human life, to the preservation of human dignity and to the safeguarding of all human rights. An experience in ordered freedom is truly a cherished part of this land" (John Paul II, "The Miami Meeting with President Reagan," *Origins*, 24 September 1987, p. 238).

9. In his Christmas message of 1944, Pius XII declared that "the democratic form of government appears to many as a postulate of nature imposed by reason itself" because democracy guarantees the citizen the right "to express his own views of the duties and sacrifices that are imposed on him" and the right not to be "compelled to obey without being heard." The peoples of Europe, "taught by bitter experience, . . . are more aggressive in opposing the concentration of dictatorial power that cannot

ris, are there approximations.[10] More clearly than his predecessors, John Paul II has defined the *institutional structures* that best secure a Jewish-Christian vision of human rights and the dignity of the person. In sum, John Paul II's first contribution in *Sollicitudo* lies in his especially acute sense of the role of certain specific institutions in protecting basic human rights. His second lies in making central to his thought the most universal of starting places, the story of Creation in Genesis.

Progress Beyond Populorum Progressio

In order to make John Paul II's theoretical and institutional advances plainer, we do well to look again at the encyclical whose anniversary he is celebrating. *Populorum Progressio* was issued fifteen months after the conclusion of the Second Vatican Council. At the Council, the great panorama of Catholic bishops of all races from what was then just beginning to be called the "Third World" came for the first time into the full view of the fascinated public. (Compare the seven hundred bishops at Vatican I in 1870 to the twenty-two hundred at Vatican II in 1961.) Heretofore, "Catholic social teaching" had been centrally addressed to the problems of industrialization, and especially to the workers of Europe.[11] The Church and its terminology were Eurocentric, and

---

be censured or touched, and call for a system of government more in keeping with the dignity and liberty of the citizens. . . . These multitudes . . . are today firmly convinced . . . that had there been the possibility of censuring and correcting the actions of public authority, the world would not have been dragged into the vortex of a disastrous war, and that to avoid for the future the repetition of such a catastrophe we must vest efficient guarantees in the people itself." See also Guido Gonella, *The Papacy and World Peace* (London: Hollis and Carter, 1945).

10. In *Pacem in Terris*, 8-26, John XXIII gives his own Bill of Rights, which includes the right to life, the right to free inquiry, to worship, to work, to private property, to free association, to emigrate and immigrate, to equal protection of the laws, etc.

11. Joseph Gremillion writes: "Before the aggiornamento, Catholic social teaching addressed itself almost exclusively to the North Atlantic region, the nations that first experienced the Industrial Revolution. Indeed, original reflection on the Gospel, Church, and modern economic power was concentrated within a small oblong diamond whose points reach ap-

America was largely out of focus, dim on the periphery. Such terms as "liberal" were employed in the sense that they had acquired on the European continent: anti-Catholic, radically antireligious, atheistic, and materialistic. Although "Manchester liberals" were occasionally mentioned (by Pius XI, e.g.), this reference appears to have been derived from a group of German economists who used that name.[12]

Between 1947 and Vatican II, meanwhile, Europe had already experienced the "European miracle" of swift political and economic recovery through the combination of democratic institutions and a modified capitalism which the Germans call the "social market economy." But during the Council, the attention of the Church was jolted by the comparative economic stagnation of Latin America, Africa, and Asia. This is the problem that Paul VI addressed in *Populorum Progressio*. He had become the first "pilgrim pope," and had been deeply impressed, as he notes, by what he had seen on his worldwide trips.[13]

Consider the situation when Paul VI wrote that encyclical in 1967. The capital stock of Japan had been all but leveled in World War II, an unnecessary war into which unchecked war lords had led a great nation. By 1967, Japan had already recovered dramatically; but it was still far from being the economic giant that it was to become during the next twenty years. In 1967, South Korea was far poorer than any nation in Latin America, and Taiwan, Hong Kong, and Singapore still ranked among very poor developing nations. In 1965, life expectancy in Latin America as a whole was 57 years; in Africa, 42 years; and in Asia 44

---

proximately Paris, Brussels, Munich, and Milan" ("Overview and Prospectus," in Gremillion, ed., *The Gospel of Peace and Justice: Catholic Social Teaching since Pope John* [Maryknoll, New York: Orbis Books, 1976], p. 35).

12. See my discussion of "The 'Manchester Liberals'" in *Freedom with Justice: Catholic Social Thought and Liberal Institutions* (San Francisco: Harper & Row, 1984), pp. 81-87.

13. "Before We became Pope, two journeys, to Latin America in 1960 and to Africa in 1962, brought Us into direct contact with the acute problems pressing on continents full of life and hope. Then on becoming Father of all We made further journeys to the Holy Land and India, and were able to see and virtually touch the very serious difficulties besetting peoples of long-standing civilizations who are at grips with the problem of development" (Pope Paul VI, *Populorum Progressio*, 4).

years. (By 1985, these crucial numbers would advance to 64 years, 51 years, and 52 years, respectively.)[14] Seeing the misery, even as populations were beginning to experience advances in hygiene and health, Paul VI began with a lapidary phrase: For him, the "principal fact" of 1967 was that "the social question has become worldwide" (4).

Thus did Pope Paul VI bring the Catholic Church face-to-face with the reality that Adam Smith had been the first to articulate in 1776: the possibility, and therefore the moral duty, that all the nations of the world could break out from the age-old prison that poverty had imposed upon the human race, through a systematic inquiry into the nature and causes of the wealth of nations. (Leo XIII had already alluded to *The Wealth of Nations* in *Rerum Novarum* in 1891.)[15] Nearly thirty years earlier, by contrast, Pope Pius IX had issued his *Syllabus of Errors*, hurling at Continental liberalism such anathemas as: "The Roman Pontiff can and ought to reconcile himself to, and agree with, progress, liberalism and recent civilization."[16] Against development, the Church seemed then to have shut its door. Leo XIII opened it by more than a crack. But Paul VI, following Vatican II, was now willing to walk through it, saying in one of the most famous lines of *Populorum Progressio*: "Development is the new name for peace" (87).

Literally, of course, this statement is not true. The pursuit of justice is more often like a flaming sword. New standards of health and medicine mean bulging populations. Premodern institutions strain under modern dynamisms. Economic, political, and cultural development imposes a new set of moral obligations. Most of all, once the secrets of how to create wealth in a systematic fashion have been discerned, then poverty is no longer morally acceptable. Given the suffering imposed by the ancient prison of poverty, *the new moral obligation is development*. Morally, if we can lift the siege of immemorial poverty by creating new

---

14. U.N. Department of International Economic and Social Affairs, *Demographic Indicators of Countries* (New York: United Nations, 1982).

15. See Oswald von Nell-Breuning, *Reorganization of the Social Economy: The Social Encyclical Developed and Explained* (New York: Bruce Publishing Co., 1936), p. 131.

16. Quoted in Newman C. Eberhardt, *A Summary of Catholic History*, vol. 2 (St. Louis: Herder, 1962), p. 467.

wealth on a worldwide basis, among all peoples, we must do so. No national leader can any longer say: "My people are a poor people; and we intend to keep them that way." Development, in sum, is a new moral obligation. Turmoil, not peace, is the first result, although not the hoped-for and ultimate result.

Thus, Adam Smith launched a process that would inspire the entire world to undertake a three-hundred-year journey toward developing the wealth of every nation. Obviously, not every people would choose to proceed at the same pace. Indeed, the burden of Smith's argument was that many of the experiments in "the Colonies" (soon to become the United States) were in advance of those of Great Britain. He argued that Great Britain should learn from these experiments, and break the stranglehold of state mercantilism that was keeping Britons far poorer than they ought to be. In this long historical process, he thought, one nation should learn from another. The new art of "political economy," of which Smith is justly called the founder, was in his mind empirical, rooted in experience, corrigible by trial and error. He himself ransacked the world (much of his book is about practices in what we would today call the "Third World") for examples and lessons. And he by no means thought that development should be economic solely. He was a moral philosopher by training, of an unusually empirical bent, and shared a Protestant-Christian sense of "moral sentiments" and communitarian values.[17]

---

17. Robert N. Bellah recently wrote that "there is a benign, optimistic, and profoundly moral quality to Adam Smith's notion of the invisible hand that was transformed almost into its opposite in the gloomy amoral scientism of Malthus's iron laws." Smith's defense of the free market, Bellah adds, "was based on his belief in the virtues of the 'system of natural liberty' that it embodied. Yet much as Smith admired the effectiveness of the self-regarding virtues in contributing to a productive economy, he never imagined that they were superior to the other-regarding virtues" (Bellah, "The Economics Pastoral, A Year Later," *Commonweal*, 18 December 1987). Gertrude Himmelfarb has influenced Bellah in this area. She writes: "For Smith political economy was not an end in itself but a means to an end, that end being the wealth and well-being, moral and material, of the 'people,' of whom the 'laboring poor' were the largest part" (*The Idea of Poverty: England in the Early Industrial Age* [New York: Knopf, 1984], chap. 2, "Adam Smith: Political Economy as Moral Philosophy," p. 63).

This vein in Anglo-American thought is made more explicit by Paul VI: "Development cannot be limited to mere economic growth" (14). Pope Paul VI cites *The Conditions of Economic Progress*, by the lay Catholic economist Colin Clark of Australia (a nation in "the South" that early developed far beyond "Third World" status), and quotes directly from Father Lebret's work on the dynamic of human development:

> We do not believe in separating the economic from the human, nor development from the civilizations in which it exists. What we hold important is man, each man and each group of men, and we even include the whole of humanity.[18]

This was Adam Smith's point in addressing *all* nations.

"Increased possession is not the ultimate goal of nations," Paul VI writes, "nor of individuals. All growth is ambivalent" (19). Adam Smith and the other pioneers in the new science of political economics hoped to provide new ways of discerning in advance some of the consequences of various courses of action. Theirs, they accepted, was only a "dismal science" of means and probable consequences. It would have to be employed in the light of moral criteria supplied by sources beyond themselves. Quite self-consciously, the first political economists of Anglo-American background conceived of their discipline as a handmaiden of morals and ethics.[19]

---

18. *Populorum Progressio*, 14, quoting Louis Lebret, *Dynamique concrète du développement* (Paris: Economie et Humanisme, Les Editions Ouvrières, 1961), p. 28.

19. Adam Smith subordinates political economy to the prudential judgment of the legislator: "Political economy, considered as a branch of the science of a statesman or legislator, proposes two distinct objects; first, to provide a plentiful revenue or subsistence for the people, or more properly to enable them to provide such a revenue or subsistence for themselves; and secondly, to supply the state or commonwealth with a revenue sufficient for the publick services" (*An Inquiry into the Nature and Causes of the Wealth of Nations*, ed. R. H. Campbell, A. S. Skinner, and W. B. Todd, 2 vols. [Indianapolis, Indiana: Liberty Classics, 1981], book 4, "Of Systems of Political Economy," p. 428). But "it is not so with the distribution of wealth." The "opinions and feelings of mankind" determine the distribution of wealth and are part of "a far larger and more difficult subject of inquiry than political economy" (Mill, *Principles of Political Economy*, ed. Sir William Ashley [London: Longmans, Green & Co., 1909; reprint ed., Fairfield, New Jersey: August M. Kelley, 1976], book 2, chap. 1, sec. 1, pp. 199-200).

"All social action involves a doctrine," Paul VI writes. He does not say this only to separate his own vision of development from those "based upon a materialistic and atheistic philosophy . . . which [does not] respect . . . human freedom and dignity" (39). He says it, expressly, in order to promote "a new humanism." Here Paul VI specifically footnotes Jacques Maritain's *Integral Humanism*. In a later book, Maritain wrote that his vision of a humanistic future is best approximated by the example of the United States, a country whose institutions he had learned to love during his wartime exile and afterwards.[20]

Some commentators think that Paul VI has words about property that liberals find hard to swallow. For example, these: "Private property does not constitute for anyone an absolute and unconditioned right," and again: "The right to property must never be exercised to the detriment of the common good" (23). But compare those sentences to John Locke:

> labor being the unquestionable property of the laborer, no man but he can have a right to what that is once joined to, *at least where there is enough, and as good left in common for others*.[21]

---

20. See *Populorum Progressio*, n. 44. In 1958, Maritain wrote: "I would like to refer to one of my books, *Humanisme Intégral*, which was published twenty years ago. When I wrote this book, trying to outline a concrete historical ideal suitable to a new Christian civilization, my perspective was definitely European. I was in no way thinking in American terms, I was thinking especially of France, and of Europe, and of their historical problems, and of the kind of concrete prospective image that might inspire the activity, in the temporal field, of the Catholic youth of my country.

"The curious thing in this connection is that, fond as I may have been of America as soon as I saw her, and probably because of the particular perspective in which *Humanisme Intégral* was written, it took a rather long time for me to become aware of the kind of congeniality which existed between what is going on in this country and a number of views I had expressed in my book.

"Of course the book is concerned with a concrete historical ideal which is far distant from any present reality. Yet, what matters to me is the *direction* of certain essential trends characteristic of American civilization. And from this point of view I may say that *Humanisme Intégral* appears to me now as a book which had, so to speak, an affinity with the American climate by anticipation" (Jacques Maritain, *Reflections on America* [New York: Charles Scribner's Sons, 1958], pp. 174-75. Italics his).

21. John Locke, *Second Treatise*, 27 (emphasis added). Locke adds: "The same Law of Nature, that does by this means give us Property, does

And to John Stuart Mill:

> The justification, in an economical point of view, of property
> in land . . . [is] only valid, in so far as the proprietor of land is
> its improver. Whenever, in any country, the proprietor, gener-
> ally speaking, ceases to be the improver, political economy has
> nothing to say in defense of landed property, as there estab-
> lished. . . . When the "sacredness of property" is talked of, it
> should always be remembered, that any such sacredness does
> not belong in the same degree to landed property. No man
> made the land. It is the original inheritance of the whole spe-
> cies. Its appropriation is wholly a question of general expedi-
> ency. When private property in land is not expedient, it is un-
> just.[22]

For Adam Smith, "the cause of the wealth of nations" is intelligence, research, and discovery, combined with a will to ex-
plore new horizons and to take risks. The source of wealth, in
short, is human creativity. Paul VI clearly understands this, for
he writes:

> By persistent work and use of his intelligence man gradually
> wrests nature's secrets from her and finds a better application
> for her riches. As his self-mastery increases, he develops a taste
> for research and discovery, an ability to take a calculated risk,
> boldness in enterprise, generosity in what he does and a sense
> of responsibility. (25)

But, then, in his famous paragraph 26, Paul VI defines what
he calls "unchecked liberalism," which Pius XI in 1931 had de-
nounced as "the international imperialism of money." That year
was the slough of the Depression, and Hitler was on his way to
seizing power in Germany. Many "liberal" nations were soon to
fall under Axis control, and the others, especially Britain, were
mortally threatened. Notwithstanding the later liberation of

---

also *bound* that *Property* too. God *has given us all things richly*, 1 Tim. vi.
17, is the Voice of Reason confirmed by Inspiration. But how far has he
given it us? To enjoy. As much as any one can make use of to any advantage of life before it spoils; so much he may by his labor fix a Property in.
Whatever is beyond this, is more than his share, and belongs to others.
Nothing was made by God for Man to spoil or destroy" (ibid., 31; emphasis in original).

22. Mill, *Principles of Political Economy*, book 2, chap. 2, sec. 6, pp. 231,
233.

Europe, and notwithstanding the "miraculous" development of Europe after World War II, Paul VI then defines "unchecked liberalism" in terms that no liberal society of 1967 actually embodied. He means by "unchecked liberalism" a system "which considers profit as the key motive for economic progress, competition as the supreme law of economics, and private ownership of the means of production as an absolute right that has no limits and carries no corresponding social obligation." One year before Leo XIII wrote *Rerum Novarum*, economic historian Stephen T. Worland notes, the Sherman Anti-Trust Act (not to mention social legislation since) made this definition inapplicable to realities in the United States.[23] In the light of universal sin, liberalism like everything else is properly given check.

Another famous sentence opens paragraph 66: "The world is sick." Its illness, says the pope, lies chiefly in "the lack of brotherhood among individuals and peoples." A moment later, he calls upon Western "industrialists, merchants, leaders or representatives of larger enterprises." First he commends their virtue at home, then upbraids their vices abroad: "It happens that they are not lacking in social sensitivity in their own country; why then do they return to the inhuman principles of individualism when they operate in less developed countries?" (70) In this and in many other passages, the encyclical overlooks the difference between the *systems* of developed nations and those of undeveloped nations. Virtue without institutions is seldom sufficient. To support virtue and to restrain vice, well-designed checks and balances are necessary. Individuals can

---

23. "Now it is obvious, given the existence of the Sherman Act and the way Section 1 has been enforced, that Pope Paul's definition of liberal capitalism is grossly inaccurate as a description of the U.S. economic system. For the Sherman Act clearly forbids some kinds of profit seeking. And it is certainly not the case that in our system 'private ownership . . . carries no social obligation.' The history of the Sherman Act shows that a business executive who uses his property to form a cartel—who flouts his social obligation by violating Section 1—will be put in jail. There may be somewhere in the world, somewhere in history, economic systems that tolerate the crude individualism stigmatized by Pope Paul VI. But the record shows the U.S. economy is not one of them" (Stephen T. Worland, "The Preferential Option for the Poor: An Economist's Perspective," Inaugural Lecture of the William and Virginia Clemens Chair, St. John's University, Collegeville, 23 October 1987 [pamphlet]).

scarcely function in the same way in one set of institutions as in another.

Poorly designed systems quite often frustrate virtuous persons, whereas well-designed institutions make even less virtuous persons function better than they otherwise might. From Poland Father Jozef Tischner gives examples concerning the frustration of Polish fishermen, who labor at risk to life and limb, only to learn that their catch frequently rots in ill-kept refrigerated warehouses, under the management of incompetent authorities.[24] Suppliers of public transport in Lima, Peru, 95 percent of whom are working as "illegals," cannot gain legal incorporation papers, obtain legitimate credit, or qualify for insurance; they must labor uneasily outside the law.[25] Consider, too, a virtuous family in Argentina trying to save funds for their children's education as the inflation of 1985 reached more than 100 percent *per month*. Morally, should such a family invest those funds in Argentina? If they do, at that rate of inflation, their children will not be able to afford higher education. If with many others they do not, Argentina will lose its sources of internal in-

---

24. Father Tischner, reported to be one of the authors of *Sollicitudo*, writes of Poland: "What good does it do when a fisherman exceeds a quota if there is no place to store the excess fish? What good does it do when people build a steel mill if the steel produced in it is more expensive and of poorer quality than the steel available on the open market? This . . . kind of betrayal consists in condemning work to senselessness" (*The Spirit of Solidarity*, trans. Marek B. Zaleski and Benjamin Fiore [New York: Harper & Row, 1984], p. 86).

25. Peruvian novelist Mario Vargas Llosa writes: "In Lima alone, informal commerce (excluding manufacturing) provides work for some 445,000 people. Of the 331 markets in the city, 274 (83 percent) have been constructed by informals. With regard to transport, it is no exaggeration to say that the inhabitants of Lima can move around the city thanks to the informals since, according to the findings of the Institute for Liberty and Democracy, 95 percent of the public transportation system of Lima belongs to them. Informals have invested more than $1 billion in the vehicles and maintenance facilities. . . . Half of the population of Lima lives in homes constructed by informals. Between 1960 and 1984 the state built low income housing at a cost of $173.6 million. In the same period, the informals built homes for the incredible sum of $8.2 billion (forty-seven times more than the state)" ("Peru's Silent Revolution," *Crisis*, July-August 1987, pp. 4-5, from the introduction to Hernando de Soto, *El Otro Sendero: La Revolucion Informal*. English translation forthcoming).

vestment, and will not be able to develop. Individuals cannot escape the realities of the institutions in which they must live and work.

I have written in greater detail about *Populorum Progressio* in my study of Catholic social thought, *Freedom With Justice*.[26] The judgment made there seems to me to be confirmed by events. Let us now look at the steps beyond Paul VI taken by John Paul II, especially in economics.

Creation Theology

Sollicitudo is divided into seven parts. Let us highlight important points in each, in turn. (In what follows, italics within quotes are those of the encyclical. For the most part, quotations are in the sequence of their appearance. Numbers in parentheses indicate the section in which quotations appear.)

His introduction repeatedly alerts us that, while maintaining continuity with the past, Pope John Paul II intends to say something "new." He grants that *Populorum Progressio* retains its force as "an *appeal to conscience*" (italics in original), but John Paul II wants to extend its impact and bring it to bear upon 1987, not 1967. For time passes *"ever more quickly"* today, and "the *configuration of the world* in the course of the last twenty years . . . has undergone notable changes and presents some totally new aspects." John Paul's emphasis is upon the new. *Progressio*, in his view, is dated. Indeed, "the aim of the present *reflection* is to emphasize, through a theological investigation of the present world, the need for a fuller and more nuanced concept of development" (4). A fuller and more nuanced concept—that is the aim.

In part II, John Paul II credits Paul VI with three points of originality. In each case except the last, though, John Paul II highly qualifies that originality. First, Paul VI addressed an *economic* and *social* problem in a *theological, papal* way; but Leo XIII, John Paul notes, had already done this in 1891. Second, Paul VI asserted that "the social question is now worldwide"; but "in

---

26. See Novak, *Freedom with Justice*, chap. 7, "The Development of Nations: John XXIII and Paul VI," pp. 133-40.

fact," *Sollicitudo* notes, Pope John XXIII "had already entered into this wider outlook" six years earlier (9). This is faint praise.

The third point of originality is the one Pope John Paul II develops. He chooses as a summary of *Populorum Progressio:* "Development is the new name for peace," and says that, if this is true, "war and military preparations are the major enemy of the integral development of peoples" (10). This does not appear to be an empirical claim. No evidence for it is produced, nor are various forms of apparently contradictory evidence addressed. So the words need to be examined closely.

In the war between Iran and Iraq, for example, development *has* been interrupted by awful war. Yet during the two decades 1947-1967 Western Europe and Japan had by a political, economic, and cultural "miracle" leapt far beyond the poverty and misery to which World War II had reduced them. Had they not resisted Soviet expansion, however, could they have done so? *Despite* the burden of "military preparedness," they had developed far beyond their prewar state. They also developed far beyond the laggard nations of the Third World, many of whom had escaped the destruction of World War II entirely. To offer another example: despite the heavy burden of military preparedness imposed upon South Korea by the unrelenting bellicosity of its Communist neighbor to the north (whose government did not scruple to set off a bomb in Burma in 1983 to kill as many of the South Korean cabinet as its agents could), South Korea has developed with remarkable rapidity during the years 1967-1987.

Clearly, Pope John Paul II's intention here is *not* to set forth empirically all the factual materials relating "war and military preparedness" to "development," materials which are almost as various as the nations. His is a more commonsense point. Wouldn't it be morally better if the resources currently going into arms would go into ending poverty worldwide? Would that no arms were necessary! Would that all citizens could be involved in peaceful human commerce and cultural interchange! Would that there were no Berlin Wall separating the two branches of Europe! No doubt, too, the pope hopes to speed the "liberalization" of the USSR along, so that that Wall will come down. (It is noteworthy that in China, the USSR, and nearly all other places, although not in papal documents, "liberal" has become a positive word. The history of the word "liberal" in Italy may supply clues to the Vatican's special usage.)[27]

In part III, John Paul II offers his "Survey of the Contemporary World." The "*first fact*" he notes is that "the *hopes for development*, at that time [1967] so lively, today appear very far from being realized." Paul VI had "no illusions," John Paul II says. Elsewhere, though, "there was a *certain* widespread *optimism*" about development. If Paul had no illusions, John Paul admits to "a *rather negative* impression" of "the present situation of the world." He writes: "Without going into an analysis of figures and statistics," it is sufficient to point to the multitudes suffering from "the intolerable burden of poverty" (12-13). His intention is expressly not analytical, nor empirical even, but rather to come to the moral point.

His "*first negative observation*" concerns "the persistence and often the widening of the *gap*" between the developed and the developing nations. "Gap" is "perhaps . . . not the appropriate word," he notes, since the reality is not "*stationary*" but has to do with "the *pace of progress*." (Actually, the pace of economic growth is often *higher* in Third-World countries. But even when some attain a 10-percent annual growth, versus 1 percent in developing nations, this results arithmetically in a wider gap.)[28] The pope recognizes the inadequacy of the word "gap." The

---

27. For an extended contrast between Italian liberalism and Anglo-American liberalism, see E. E. Y. Hales, *Pio Nono* (Garden City, New York: Image Books, 1962); see also Hales, *The Church in the Modern World: A Survey from the French Revolution to the Present* (Garden City, New York: Image Books, 1960). Perhaps in recognition of this contrast, the Italian text of *Sollicitudo* avoids the positive word *liberale*, preferring the pejorative *liberista*; the latter refers to a materialistic, highly egocentric, and anti-Catholic form of Latin libertarianism. A similar history supplies negative connotations for "liberal" in Latin America.

28. Marc Plattner has described the pitfalls of concentrating on the "gap" between developed and developing nations. For example, according to a World Bank study, "*despite the unprecedentedly high growth rates of the industrialized countries, there was a slight narrowing of the relative gap from 1950 to 1975.*" But, "while the developing countries were succeeding in narrowing the relative gap during the 1970s, their per capita GNP was growing at a *slower* rate than it had during the 1960s (when the gap had been widening)" ("Thinking about the 'North-South Gap,'" *This World*, Winter 1984, p. 26; emphasis in original).

point he wishes to make is not the arithmetic one; his point is the prolonged suffering of the poor. Why does it happen? He turns quickly to "the *differences of culture* and *value systems* between the various population groups . . . which help to create distances" (14). This is an important economic point. The habits of people do differ, with enormous economic consequences. Consider the Chinese, a successful subculture wherever they go. Consider the percentage of gross world product that the roughly 120 million Japanese of 1980 produced, compared to that produced by the roughly 120 million Brazilians.[29] Differences of culture and value systems do make an economic difference.

Then come two passages of extraordinary originality in papal teaching. John Paul II speaks first of "a right which is important not only for the individual but also for the common good." Yet, "in today's world . . . [this] *right of economic initiative* is often suppressed." This *"right of economic initiative"* becomes central to the rest of the document, the linchpin of John Paul II's theological vision of a good economic order. He grounds "the spirit of initiative" in *"the creative subjectivity of the citizen."* (Each citizen is made in the image of the Creator.) Moreover, the pope sees that this right serves both the *common good* and the human spirit. His primary justification for it is a common good argument. He contrasts respect for it with its suppression, and rests his case on experience.

> Experience shows us that the denial of this right, or its limitation in the name of an alleged "equality" of everyone in society, diminishes, or in practice absolutely destroys the spirit of initiative, that is to say *the creative subjectivity of the citizen*. As a consequence, there arises, not so much a true equality as a "leveling down." In the place of creative initiative there appears passivity, dependence and submission to the bureaucratic apparatus which, as the only "ordering" and "decision-making" body—if not also the "owner"—of the entire totality of goods and the means of production, puts everyone in a position of almost absolute dependence, which is similar to the

29. In 1980, Japan and Brazil contained 2.6 percent and 2.7 percent of the world's population, respectively. But Japan produced 9 percent of world gross national product, while Brazil produced only 2 percent (U.S. Central Intelligence Agency, National Foreign Assessment Center, *Handbook of Economic Statistics* [Washington, D.C.: U.S. Government Printing Office, 1981], figure 1).

traditional dependence of the worker-proletarian in capitalism. This provokes a sense of frustration or desperation and
predisposes people to opt out of national life, impelling many
to emigrate and also favoring a form of "psychological" emigration. (15)

This passage is a silver spike in the heart of Marxism-Leninism.

The second vital point made by John Paul II in this section re-
defines poverty. Deprivation of material goods is bad; but "in
today's world there are many other *forms of poverty.*" In some
ways, the denial of rights of the spirit is a worse form of poverty
than material deprivation.

The denial or limitation of human rights—as for example the
right to religious freedom, the right to share in the building of
society, the freedom to organize and to form unions, or to take
initiatives in economic matters—do these not impoverish the
human person as much as, if not more than, the deprivation of
material goods? And is development which does not take into
account the full affirmation of these rights really development
on the human level? (15)

This is another silver spike to the heart.

Since 1967, John Paul II judges, "conditions have become *notably worse.*" In this summary judgment, the pope is obviously
discounting certain achievements, since he mentions elsewhere
that some developing nations (India is one) have "gained *self-
sufficiency in food*" (26). He could have mentioned, but did not,
that levels of longevity and higher education are advancing
strikingly, and that advances in health and longevity are better
indices of development than many others.[30] Again a number of
nations poor in 1967 rank today among the developed countries
(several nations of East Asia among them). Still, he discerns
"various causes" for the "deterioration" he observes. The first
is "undoubtedly grave omissions on the part of the developing
nations themselves." The second is that developed nations
"have not always, at least in due measure, felt the duty" to help
less affluent countries (16).

In particular, he discerns—without specifics and without cit-

---

30. See Nick Eberstadt's essay in *Modern Capitalism*, vol. 2: *Capitalism
and Equality in the Third World*, ed. Peter L. Berger (Lanham, Maryland:
University Press of America, 1987).

ing evidence—"economic, financial and social *mechanisms* which, although they are manipulated by people, often function almost automatically, thus accentuating the situation of wealth for some and poverty for the rest."

The pope turns next to three *"specific signs* of underdevelopment," two of which occur even within the developed countries: the housing shortage; the "shrinking" of sources of employment; and the debt crisis of the Third World (17-19). Regarding the last, the document produced by the Pontifical Commission for Justice and Peace (27 December 1986),[31] which the pope cites, has been praised by the editorial writers of the *Wall Street Journal*. The one point the document overlooks is that many nations have borrowed huge sums ($50 billion in the case of South Korea), but used this capital so creatively that they have not only paid interest on it, and returned much of the principal ahead of schedule, but have also made a profit on it. Far from stagnating or declining, such nations have used debt to leap forward. Others, of course, have borrowed the capital of others, but put it to such uncreative use that they cannot now repay it. This is a tragedy, in whose resolution (the Institute of Justice and Peace wisely wrote) all must participate. The lending peoples have been preparing themselves to absorb considerable losses. Capital placed at risk is often, in fact, lost in that way.

Regarding the homeless, the pope has a good point, widely accepted. Regarding unemployment in the developed nations, however, he does not note that Western Europe has lost two million net jobs since 1970, whereas the United States during the same period has generated thirty-five million new jobs. (It gained 500,000 in February 1988 alone, the month in which the encyclical appeared.) The United States today has a higher proportion of adults over fifteen years of age employed (62 percent) than at any time in its history.[32] In the United States, the *"sources of work"* are plainly *not* shrinking. Most of the thirty-five million jobs were created by *small* businesses. Indeed, during 1985, some 12,500 new businesses were established during every *week*,

---

31. See Pontifical Commission, *Iustitia et Pax*, in *At the Service of the Human Community: An Ethical Approach to the International Debt Question* (Vatican City: Vatican Polyglot Press, 1986).

32. Calculated from *Economic Indicators*, January 1988, p. 11.

650,000 per year.[33] The reason for this lies in the pope's often-repeated principle: the right to private economic initiative. In Europe, by contrast, the obstacles young persons encounter in trying to start new businesses are formidable. European governments have chosen security for those already employed, and their economies have stagnated accordingly;[34] the United States has chosen the right to private economic initiative, and has thereby experienced the longest period of steady economic growth in its history.

In sections 20-23, the encyclical argues that another cause of deterioration in the developing nations is the military rivalry between the East bloc and the West bloc. Elsewhere, Peter Berger discusses this theme from an empirical point of view.[35] The pope claims to be offering a factual "Survey of the Contemporary World." Such a factual survey has no more authority than the

33. National Commission on Jobs and Small Business, "Summary of Meeting of September 10-11, 1985, Washington, D.C." (typescript).

34. Peter Drucker writes: "Big business has been losing jobs since the early '70s. . . . Nearly all job creation has been in small and medium-sized businesses, and practically all of it in entrepreneurial and innovative businesses." By contrast, "there are few signs of entrepreneurial dynamism in Western Europe" ("Why America's Got So Many Jobs," *Wall Street Journal*, 24 January 1984). The late Arthur F. Burns, former U.S. ambassador to West Germany, concurred: Largely due to tax incentives, "the spirit of risk-taking and entrepreneurship therefore remained alive in the United States. In Massachusetts, for example, which became a depressed area during the 1950s, entrepreneurially minded scientists joined venture capitalists, enterprising commercial bankers, and managerial experts in establishing and nourishing hundreds of small high-technology firms. Before many years passed, they succeeded in transforming Massachusetts into one of the most progressive parts of the American economy. . . .

"There has been no corresponding upsurge of entrepreneurship in Europe. There are many reasons why the entrepreneurial spirit is less firmly implanted in Europe. I have already alluded to some of them—the high level of taxation, the regulatory burdens, the immense power of trade unions, and the increasing share of labor in national income. . . .

"The institutional limitations on entrepreneurship in Europe are further inhibited by psychological attitudes. Investors are more fearful of failure and therefore are less inclined to take risks, and this is a major reason why Western Europe has been so deficient during the past ten to fifteen years in creating new jobs" ("The Condition of the World Economy," *AEI Economist*, June 1986, pp. 3-4).

35. See his essay in this volume.

facts warrant. As regards the "parallelism" between East and West that the Polish pope surprisingly alleges, the following brief comments are in order.

(1) These paragraphs must be read in the light of the body of the pope's earlier work. (2) The actual *praxis* of East and West must be evaluated in the light of the *moral criteria* the pope proposes for the good society. Every one of these criteria reflects basic principles of Western, but not Eastern, societies. (3) Twenty-five million Americans (one in ten) have roots in the lands under the domination of the USSR. They know well that their lands of origin do not have the same voluntary relation to the Warsaw Pact that Western nations have to NATO. They know through family experience the moral and empirical differences between life in the East and life in the West. (4) "Moral equivalence" (a phrase not used by the pope) is flatly rejected by both the Left and the Right in the United States.[36] It is common Western practice to *criticize* both West and East, although everyone knows that the act of criticism has very different consequences in each. (5) Evidence to support the claims in sections 20-23 is lacking. The lack of historical detail embodied in these passages has puzzled the pope's admirers and made many who have normally been hostile to him gleeful. (Further comments follow under "Moral Parallelism," below.)

It seems that the pope is so eager to have the wall between East and West come down, and the suffocating Iron Curtain removed, that he has permitted himself a certain rhetorical excess, in order to achieve a more liberal, open, and free international society, shaped by Western ideas of respect for such basic rights as religious liberty and the right to private economic initiative. His aim is noble. These passages, indeed, recall Alexander Solzhenitsyn's Harvard address, "A World Split Apart," in which, however, the prophetic novelist in criticizing both sides was more careful than the encyclical to avoid claims of moral parallelism.[37]

---

36. See Michael Kinsley, "Dining on Red Herrings," *Curse of the Giant Muffins and Other Washington Maladies* (New York: Summit Books, 1987). Apparently, only the editor of the *New Oxford Review* proclaims moral equivalence (editorial, April 1988).

37. Solzhenitsyn explicitly condemned moral equivalence: "Very well known representatives of your society, such as George Kennan, say: 'We cannot apply moral criteria to politics.' Thus we mix good and evil, right

"The *demographic problem*," the pope observes, cuts both ways. Some nations do suffer "difficulties" from growing populations. But "the northern hemisphere" is suffering from a *"drop in the birthrate,"* which is already having severe "repercussions on the aging of the population" (25). The pope could here have cited Ben Wattenberg's powerful study, *The Birth Dearth*.[38] Here the pope could also have made, and did not, a powerful connection between his emphasis on "the image of God," endowed in humans by their Creator, and his emphasis on the *"right of economic initiative"* (15). Each new infant is not solely an open mouth, a consumer (lowering the national per-capita income by increasing the size of the population), but also has a brain, hands, and heart able to invent and to create far more than he or she will ever consume in life. This fact, indeed, is the very ground of development. The cause of the wealth of nations is the wit (Latin, *caput*) of every single citizen. Many of the most highly developed nations (Japan, Hong Kong, the Netherlands) are among the most densely populated places on earth; many of the less developed (Brazil, e.g.) are among the least densely populated.

Next the pope turns to the *"positive aspects"* in the contemporary world, especially "the more *lively concern* that *human rights should be respected"* (26). This is a triumph for Western conceptions of human rights as natural, universal, and beyond the claims of states. He also mentions his *"ecological concern."*[39] Coming from what is one of the most polluted spots on earth, beneath the air inversion over the region of Krakow in Poland, the pope knows vividly the heavy pollution that heedless and incautious industrialization can wreak upon nature and humankind.

---

and wrong, and make space for the absolute triumph of absolute evil in the world. Only moral criteria can help the West against communism's well-planned world strategy" ("A World Split Apart," in *Solzhenitsyn at Harvard*, ed. Robert Berman [Washington, D.C.: Ethics and Public Policy Center, 1980], pp. 13-14).

38. See Ben J. Wattenberg, *The Birth Dearth: What Happens When People in Free Countries Don't Have Enough Babies?* (New York: Pharos Books, 1987).

39. For example, the pope writes that "the direct or indirect result of industrialization is, ever more frequently, the pollution of the environment, with serious consequences for the health of the population" (*Sollicitudo Rei Socialis*, 34).

Finally, the pope also recognizes that certain "Third World" countries, "despite the burden of many negative factors, have succeeded in reaching a *certain self-sufficiency in food*, or a degree of industrialization which makes it possible to survive with dignity and to guarantee sources of employment for the active population" (26). Since these achievements flow from the pope's stated moral principles, especially from respect for the right to private economic initiative, we may hope that in a later encyclical the pope will reflect upon the nature and causes of these success stories, amid his generally negative impressions about the current situation.

The History of Liberty

Philosophically and theologically, chapter IV on "Authentic Human Development" is the heart of this encyclical. Here the pope turns to theology as story. He roots this story in the Creation story of Genesis. He says, "A part of this divine plan . . . *is our own history*, marked by our personal and collective effort to raise up the human condition." In this great story, the Church plays a role, has "a *duty*," and urges "all to think about the nature and characteristics of authentic human development" (31). This last point establishes a large agenda for the future.

Development, the pope begins, "*is not* a straightforward process, *as it were automatic* and *in itself limitless*" (27). Plainly, "the *mere accumulation* of goods and services, even for the benefit of the majority, is not enough for the realization of human happiness." In this light, he criticizes "a form of *superdevelopment*, equally inadmissible . . . which consists in an *excessive* availability of every kind of material goods," which "easily makes people slaves of 'possession' and of immediate gratification." This is a theme that many Americans welcome. Most of us are fond of criticizing our own civilization in this respect, and in denouncing with the pope "the so-called civilization of 'consumption' or 'consumerism,' which involves so much 'throwing-away' and 'waste.'" Those who live that way suffer, just as the pope says, "a *radical dissatisfaction*" (28). Materialism is not satisfying. Humans do not live by material things alone.

The pope points out that "having" is necessary for "being."

It is wrong that some are "deprived of essential goods" and so "do not succeed in realizing their basic human vocation." Others who have much, caught by "the cult of 'having'" do not "really succeed in 'being'." We must see material goods as "a gift from God." More than that, "the danger of the misuse of material goods and the appearance of artificial needs should in no way hinder the regard we have for the new goods and resources placed at our disposal and the use we make of them." Being made in God's image, we have a special relation to "the *earth*, from which God forms man's body, and the *breath of life* which he breathes into man's nostrils" (cf. Gen. 2:7). Economic development, therefore, is *"necessary,"* but not sufficient. It is *"necessary, . . .* since it must supply the greatest possible number of the world's inhabitants with an availability of goods essential for them 'to be'." This is a nice revision of the Benthamite calculus: "The greatest good for the greatest number." The "notion of development," then, is not only a profane notion, but "the *modern expression* of an essential dimension of man's vocation" (28-30).

"The fact is that man was not created, so to speak, immobile and static" (30). Humans have a vocation to pursue development. As Romano Guardini used to say, the liturgy is "all creation, redeemed and at prayer." The human vocation is to bring creation to its preordained fruition, to discover, to create. The pope's Genesis view of the world brings the Catholic Church into the world of progress and development—with an acute sense of sin, human fragility, and the need for mercy (the subject of the pope's second encyclical).[40]

The pope is far from being entirely pessimistic. "The story of the human race described by Sacred Scripture is, even after the fall into sin, a story of *constant achievements* . . . today's 'development' is to be seen as a moment in the story which began at creation, a story which is constantly endangered by reason of infidelity to the Creator's will, and especially by the temptation to idolatry." Development is a *"difficult yet noble task,"* in which "it is always man who is the protagonist" (30). One wishes that in a future encyclical, the pope will humbly admit that many of those who first dreamed of development found the Catholic

---

40. See Pope John Paul II, "Dives in Misericordia," *Origins*, 11 December 1980.

Church (and other churches of their time) rather unsympathetic and undiscerning. For, even explicitly, John Paul II admits to re-appropriating their dream, but now within a new horizon:

> Here the perspectives widen. The dream of "unlimited prog-ress" reappears, radically transformed by the *new outlook* created by Christian faith. (31)

In the *Federalist*, Madison and Hamilton wrote so often in a pessimistic vein of the sinfulness that humans have shown throughout recorded history, that finally in number 76 Hamil-ton feels obliged to correct the balance by showing that, none-theless, humans do often rise above their faults to perform nobly and to secure the common good.[41] Similarly, John Paul II, having sounded many "pessimistic" notes, as he admits, turns now to correct the balance.

The pope cites the *"optimistic vision* of history and work, that is to say of the *perennial value* of authentic human achieve-ments," often found in the Fathers of the Church. He explicitly commends Saint Basil the Great, Theodoret of Cyr, and Saint Augustine's *City of God*, Book XIX (31 in n. 58).

The pope turns again to liberty, stressing that the develop-ment of peoples or nations "should also include individual cul-tural identity and openness to the transcendent. Not even the need for development can be used as an excuse for imposing on others one's own way of life or own religious belief" (32). This passage offers important support for systems of pluralism and liberty of conscience. He emphasizes that "The *intrinsic connec-tion* between authentic development and respect for human rights once again reveals the *moral* character of development," especially as regards "each individual." Development that does not respect spiritual requirements "will prove unsatisfying and in the end contemptible" (33).

Toward the end, the pope links *solidarity* and *freedom* in a most important way. (In *Freedom With Justice*, I pointed out that "free-dom" is essential to the Catholic concept of social justice—that

---

41. Hamilton writes: "The supposition of universal venality in human nature is little less an error in political reasoning than the supposition of universal rectitude. The institution of delegated power implies that there is a portion of virtue and honor among mankind, which may be a rea-sonable foundation of confidence" (*Federalist* 76).

"justice" and "peace" alone are not enough. The Lay Commission on Catholic Social Thought and the U.S. Economy also stressed that, without "freedom," the concept of "solidarity" may suggest the suppression of dissent, lack of liberty, etc.)[42] The pope writes, "In order to be genuine, development must be achieved within the framework of *solidarity* and *freedom*, without ever sacrificing either of them under whatever pretext" (33).

Finally, in section 34, the pope turns again to ecology, making three comments: Humans must "take into account *the nature of each being* and of its *mutual connection* in an ordered system." Second, "*natural resources* are limited; some are not, as it is said, *renewable*." Third, the result of industrialization must not be "the pollution of the environment" (34). All these are today part of the secular conventional wisdom of the West. The City of Pittsburgh, where I partially grew up, was then one of the nation's most polluted cities, and is now one of the cleanest.

On these points, the pope is here factually inexact only about "limits" on natural resources. The fundamental natural resource is the human mind.[43] "Resources" are constantly changing, as the mind finds better substitutes for older materials. Fiber optics are replacing copper in lines of communication; plastics and ceramics are replacing steel in many automobile parts; electronic power is replacing mechanical power. For thousands of years oil was not a resource useful to humankind; since 1853, and for a time, it is; and now new substitutes are being sought for it. And so on. The pope's case about the moral and *spiritual* dimension of progress points in fact to the creative power of the human mind, made in the image of God. The human mind was created so that it might discern ever *new* resources, and bring them forth from the ample treasury that the Creator entrusted to human-

---

42. See Lay Commission on Catholic Social Teaching and the U.S. Economy, *Toward the Future* (Lanham, Maryland: University Press of America, 1984); *Liberty and Justice for All: Report on the Final Draft of the U.S. Catholic Bishops' Pastoral Letter* (Notre Dame, Indiana: Brownson Institute, 1986).

43. See Julian L. Simon, *The Ultimate Resource* (Princeton, New Jersey: Princeton University Press, 1981); Julian L. Simon and Herman Kahn, eds., *The Resourceful Earth: A Response to Global 2000* (London: Basil Blackwell, 1984); Max Singer, *Passage to a Human World* (Indianapolis, Indiana: Hudson Institute, 1987).

kind. Within this biosphere lie unimagined resources, appropriate to every changing era, not yet discovered.

Pope John Paul's part V, "A Theological Reading of Modern Problems," expressly goes beyond "an analysis limited exclusively to the economic and political causes of underdevelopment." He looks for *"moral causes."* He looks to "the behavior of *individuals* considered as *responsible persons."* He stresses that he is speaking in the context of "political decisions" and "political will" (35). This gives him an opportunity to repeat his opposition to a cavalier use of the expression "structures of sin" (first made in his Apostolic Exhortation *Reconciliatio et Paenitentia*).[44] Structures of sin "are rooted in personal sin, and thus always linked to the *concrete acts* of individuals." He reprints as a footnote the central passage of the Exhortation: "The real responsibility, then, lies with individuals. A situation—or, likewise, an institution, a structure, society itself—is not in itself the subject of moral acts." In other words, no one can escape personal responsibility by blaming "institutions" or "structures." To speak of "sinful structures" is to use a shorthand for the "accumulation and concentration of many *personal sins*" (36, in n. 65).

The framers of the United States Constitution recognized this very concept. Since men are not angels, Madison wrote in *Federalist* 51, government is necessary; but, then, since public officials are not exempted from the burdens of sinfulness, checks and balances are also necessary if the guardians are also to be guarded. Since institutions staffed by sinners can never be sinless; since structures are always sinful because the individuals who operate them are sinful, "ambition must be made to counteract ambition."

> This policy of supplying, by opposite and rival interests, the defect of better motives, might be traced through the whole system of human affairs, private as well as public. We see it particularly displayed in all the subordinate distributions of power, where the constant aim is to divide and arrange the several offices in such a manner as that each may be a check on the other—that the private interest of every individual may be a sentinel over the public rights.

---

44. John Paul II, "Apostolic Exhortation on Reconciliation and Penance," *Origins*, 2 December 1984.

But the obverse is also true. Given the proper checks and balances, citizens may be encouraged to act in a virtuous fashion, concerned for the common good as well as their own. Virtue is indispensable. The idea that institutions can function without virtue is "chimerical."

Next the pope diagnoses two "very typical" structures opposed to God's will:

> on the one hand, the *all-consuming desire for profit*, and on the other, *the thirst for power*, with the intention of imposing one's will upon others. In order to characterize better each of these attitudes, one can add the expression: "at any price." In other words, we are faced with the *absolutizing* of human attitudes with all its possible consequences. (37)

No one, I think, can deny that such attitudes, wherever they occur, are contrary to the will of God. In societies in which systems are divided, and powers are divided, acts of this sort are also contrary to the civil law. In such societies, moral and political institutions check and balance economic activities. Similarly, the division of powers and a great many other checks and balances within constitutional governments drastically restrict "*the thirst for power.*" In Western countries today, in fact, a more realistic question is whether political power is not too weak, too divided by checks and balances, too subject to electoral change. The United States, for example, is often accused by friends and foes of changing directions after each election. No one wishes to do away with checks and balances. Many do wonder, though, how democratic systems can prevail amid current dangers, as Jean-François Revel has written in *Why Democracies Perish*.[45]

The pope's reason for introducing these considerations seems to be to show, if I may paraphrase Charles Peguy, that "Development is moral or not at all." The path to it is "*long and complex.*" For "obstacles to integral development [the very phrase echoes Maritain's *Integral Humanism*] are not only economic but rest on *more profound attitudes* which human beings can make

---

45. See Jean-François Revel, *Why Democracies Perish*, trans. William Byron (Garden City, New York: Doubleday, 1984). See also Luigi Lombardi Vallauri and Gerhard Dilcher, eds., *Cristianesimo, Secolarizzazione e Diritto Moderno* (Milan: Giuffre Editore Milano, 1981).

into absolute values" (38). The pope, therefore, appeals to responsible persons to use their liberty with virtue. His name for
the sum of the virtues needed is "solidarity," in which each is
responsible for all, concerned for the common good for all.

> For world peace is inconceivable unless the world's leaders
> come to recognize that *interdependence* in itself demands the
> abandonment of the politics of blocs, the sacrifice of all forms
> of economic, military or political imperialism, and the trans-
> formation of mutual distrust into *collaboration*. This is pre-
> cisely the *act proper* to solidarity among individuals and na-
> tions. (39)

For the pope "*solidarity* is undoubtedly a *Christian virtue*"
(40). Even if others may not understand it in the same way,
Christians ought to exemplify it before the world. No doubt,
that is why many millions hope that the current small steps
toward the "liberalization" of the Soviet Union are not a
chimera. Not very long ago, after all, the greatest enemies of the
Western Allies were Japan and Germany. Under liberalized
governments, both those formerly Axis powers have turned
their energies to peaceful pursuits, and both have joined the
other liberal societies of the West in comity and amity. All hope
and pray that a liberalized Soviet Union, having given up its
reckless claim to world domination, will also choose the path
of development and peace, both internally and externally. The
publics of the West would, in such circumstances, be entirely
willing to join with the USSR, as during our lifetimes they have
joined with Germany and Japan. That earlier conversion is an
earnest of the conversion that yet could come. After every Mass,
not long ago, Catholics used to pray for "the conversion of Rus-
sia," as the Lady of Fatima (to whom the pope is especially
devoted) requested.

Part VI is called "Some Particular Guidelines." "The Church
does not have *technical solutions* to offer," John Paul II writes;
and it "does not propose economic and political systems or programs." There comes, then, an unbecoming boast, calculated
to make non-Catholics wince; the Church is an "expert in
humanity" (41). Most of the important practical "guidelines"
briefly mentioned by John Paul II stress the importance of freedom.

First, though, comes a very important clarification of a false interpretation that has plagued Catholic social thought for at least sixty years, a false notion to which I called attention in *Spirit of Democratic Capitalism*.[46] The pope writes:

> The Church's social doctrine *is not* a "third way" between *liberal capitalism* and *Marxist collectivism*, nor even a possible alternative to other solutions less radically opposed to one another: . . . [it is not] an *ideology*, but rather the *accurate formulation* of the results of a careful reflection on the complex realities of human existence, in society and in the international order, in the light of faith and of the church's tradition. Its main aim is to *interpret* these realities, determining their conformity with or divergence from the lines of the Gospel teaching on man and his vocation, a vocation which is at once earthly and transcendent; its aim is thus *to guide* Christian behavior. It therefore belongs to the field, not of *ideology*, but of *theology* and particularly of moral theology (41).

Next, the pope stresses the *"love of preference* for the poor," and the need for "an *international outlook*" in embracing "the immense multitudes" of those in need (42).

As a particular guideline, the pope asserts again that "the

---

46. "In a sense, by standing outside the historical stream of democratic capitalism, the popes were able to make some legitimate criticisms of abuses and errors within it, and to support many proposals for humane reforms eventually adopted by it. Yet, simultaneously, the remnants both of the medieval world and state mercantilism were crumbling all around them. Resisting socialism and standing outside democratic capitalism, Catholic social teaching laid claim to a certain neutrality—but gradually came to seem suspended in air. Catholic thought began to deal with every sort of regime, traditional and modern, even while its talk of a Catholic 'middle way' seemed empty, since there are, in fact, no existing examples of that middle way. . . .

"For this reason, perhaps, the programs of the 1940s and the 1950s in which Catholic thinkers had invested so much hope for 'the reconstruction of the social order'—Catholic Action, the Young Christian Workers, the Christian Democratic parties—achieved some notable successes but lacked the force of an alternative ideal. To be anti-communist and anti-socialist, and only halfheartedly committed to democratic capitalism, is to represent not a 'middle way' but a halfway house. Such movements collapsed of their own lack of a serious ideal" (Michael Novak, *The Spirit of Democratic Capitalism* [New York: Simon and Schuster, 1982], p. 247).

right to property is *valid and necessary*, but . . . is under a 'social mortgage,'" and falls under the principle (common to John Locke and John Stuart Mill) that "the goods of this world are *originally meant for all.*" For Locke and Mill, the practical question is, Which *social system* is more likely to develop the goods of creation for the common good? To this query, as we have seen, Pope John Paul II has already answered: a regime respecting "*the right of economic initiative.*" His answer, then, is virtually the same as Locke's and Mill's. But John Paul II carries the point well beyond the question of material poverty:

> Likewise, in this concern for the poor, one must not overlook that *special form of poverty* which consists in being deprived of fundamental human rights, in particular the right to religious freedom and also the right to freedom of economic initiative. (42)

John Paul II has been specifically commended by the *Wall Street Journal* for calling for "the *reform of the international trade system* . . . [and] a *review of the structure of existing international organizations*" (43).

Then, in section 44, the pope returns to one of his central and often-repeated themes:

> Development demands above all a spirit of initiative on the part of the countries which need it. Each of them must act in accordance with its own responsibilities, *not expecting everything* from the more favored countries, and acting in collaboration with others in the same situation. Each must discover and use to the best advantage its *own area of freedom.* . . . It is important then that as far as possible *the developing nations themselves* should favor the *self-affirmation* of each citizen, through access to a wider culture and a free flow of information.

He again points to the nations that "achieved the goal of *food self-sufficiency*" as a model for all others.

Then come two crucial clarifications of the pope's moral criteria for the good society: Democratic political institutions are a *"necessary condition and sure guarantee* of the development of 'the whole individual and of all people'" such as *"new regional organizations* inspired by criteria of *equality, freedom and participation*" (44-45).

Freedom, At Last

This long encyclical opens its final chapter with the sentence "Peoples and individuals aspire to be free." Citing Latin America, the pope adds: "This approach makes *liberation* the fundamental category and the first principle of action" (46). At last, the Church concerned with justice and peace is adding "freedom" as its "fundamental category" and "first principle." That this is done with reference to Latin America rather than to North America underlines the Vatican's delayed recognition of "ordered liberty" in the North American experience.

In the face of "the *oad experiences of recent* years" and "the *mainly negative picture* of the present moment," the pope recalls that "The Church has *confidence also in man,* though she knows the evil of which he is capable." For this section (47), there are many parallels in the *Federalist.* Here as elsewhere, North American formulations, developed from Cicero, Aristotle, and other classic sources, and tested under modern conditions, would vindicate the pope's confidence in democracy and development.

In closing, the pope writes: "I wish *to appeal* . . . to all men and women without exception." He adds that it is "appropriate to emphasize the *preeminent role* that belongs to the *laity.*" In these matters, the laity must take the lead. They must test the cutting-edge hypotheses, gain the self-correcting experience, and "think about the nature and characteristics of authentic human development" (31). They must, in short, recapitulate Adam Smith's effort, but in a Catholic framework. They must conduct a sustained *Inquiry into the Nature and Causes of the Wealth of Nations,* where wealth means not only material wealth, but also the securing of rights, especially rights of religious liberty and pluralism, and a sense of international community (solidarity) based upon respect for autonomy and free association.

"*No temporal achievement,*" the pope concludes, "is to be identified with the Kingdom of God." All such achievements are only partial, anticipatory, "imperfect and temporary." The pope entrusts to Mary, the Mother of God, his concern for all children in "this *difficult moment* of the modern world" (48-49).

Moral Parallelism

Let us return, now, to a fuller discussion of the most controversial of the pope's empirical claims about the present world. There are nine such passages, which journalists referred to as "moral parallelism" or "equidistance" or "moral equivalence." Six of them occur in part III, "Survey of the Contemporary World," and three are repeated among the descriptive materials in part V, "A Theological Reading of Modern Problems." The first six are found on six consecutive pages in sections 20-23, and the remaining three in sections 36, 37, and 39.

The main heading under which these texts fall, in the pope's words, is "the *political* causes of today's situation." The pope singles out one large generic fact: "Faced with a combination of factors which are undoubtedly complex, we cannot hope to achieve a comprehensive analysis here. However, we cannot ignore a striking fact about the *political picture* since the Second World War." He believes that this fact "has considerable impact" on development. "I am referring to the *existence of two opposing blocs*, commonly known as the East and the West." He adds in a generic euphemism, "Each of the two blocs tends to assimilate or gather around it other countries or groups of countries, to different degrees of adherence or participation" (20). That the pope does not intend to speak precisely is clear. Cardinal Lustiger of Paris has noted recently, for example, that there are more bishops for the Ukrainian rite in the United States than in the Ukraine today.[47] Most members of the Soviet bloc do not literally "gather around" the USSR; Estonia, Latvia, Lithuania, Poland, Hungary, Czechoslovakia, and many others have been conquered. They have been kept within the East bloc by force, under the explicit terms of the Brezhnev Doctrine.

The pope judges that the opposition between the blocs is at its depth "*ideological* in nature," on the basis of "two very different visions of man and of his freedom and social role." At this point, he is silent on which vision of freedom he supports, although the rest of the encyclical makes that crystal clear. "It was inevitable," he judges, that this "*ideological opposition* should evolve into a

---

47. Jean-Marie Lustiger, "Les défis du catholicisme américain," *Le Monde*, 5 July 1986.

growing *military opposition*." What sort of inevitability he has in mind is not clear. But by trying to bring about change by persuasion, he is perhaps suggesting that such opposition has been freely chosen, and so may be freely altered. Perhaps, though, he is worried that over the next two or three decades the East will come to prevail. In that case, there is not much use in throwing his support to the West. He can only try to keep certain values alive, and to hold aloft certain institutions (democracy, the right to religious liberty, the right to private initiative, etc.) as long-term ideals. Alternatively, he may see both sides as capable of a rapid evolution, and wishes to promote this possibility.

> The question naturally arises: in what way and to what extent are these two systems capable of changes and updatings such as to favor or promote a true and integral development of individuals and peoples in modern society? (21)

He thinks that "at the present time" the danger of an "*open and total* war . . . seems to have receded, yet without completely disappearing" (20).

The pope judges that "the tension *between East and West*" concerns "two *concepts* of the development of individuals and peoples." Both concepts he describes as "being imperfect and in need of radical correction" (21). The Church, he writes later, offers no "third way" between these two concepts. It does offer "guidelines" that help to form consciences (41-42). The "moral criteria" he in fact proposes do not seem to require the same degree of "radical" change in the West that they would require in the East (21). The inferred parallelism breaks down.

What especially concerns him are the "internal divisions" that this ideological opposition engenders in developing countries, "to the extent in some cases of provoking full civil war." In addition "investments and aid for development are often diverted from their proper purpose and used to sustain conflicts, apart from and in opposition to the interests of the countries that ought to benefit from them." This leads some countries to fear "falling victim to a form of neo-colonialism." The result is that the Nonaligned Nations affirm "the right of every people to its own identity, independence and security, as well as the right to share, on a basis of equality and solidarity, in the goods intended for all" (21).

This, the pope says, is "a clearer picture of the last twenty years." It shows that the conflict between East and West in the North is "an important cause of the retardation or stagnation of the South." Instead of being *"autonomous nations,"* the nations of the South became "parts of a machine, cogs on a gigantic wheel." The one example the pope gives is that the centers of communications in the North "frequently impose a distorted vision of life and of man" (22). Americans who have watched "Dynasty" and "Dallas" on overseas television concur with that. But, surely, such distortions—in television shows produced from a clearly left-wing and antibusiness point of view[48]—injure the reputation of the United States much more than they cause economic "retardation" or "stagnation" in the South. Perhaps, though, feeding the prejudices of leftists does encourage economic retardation.

The pope's words in these passages are extremely general. The variety among developing nations is staggering. Brazil is not like Bangladesh, nor is Zaire like Argentina, nor South Korea like North Korea, nor Afghanistan like Nicaragua. It is not easy to be certain which nations and which circumstances the pope has in mind. John Paul II is describing a very big picture but without detail. Even in describing the two "blocs" he does not mention obvious differences. He writes:

> Each of the two *blocs* harbors in its own way a tendency towards *imperialism*, as it is usually called, or towards forms of new-colonialism: an easy temptation to which they frequently succumb, as history, including recent history, teaches. (22)

"Each in its own way"—the *difference* is not specified. The implication is that the way of the East is not identical to that of the West. Is there a *moral* difference between these two somehow different ways? The pope does not say.

The pope blames "an unacceptably exaggerated concern *for security*." He estimates that

---

48. See S. Robert Lichter et al., *The Media Elite: America's New Power Brokers* (Bethesda, Maryland: Adler & Adler, 1986). See also Ben Stein, *The View from Sunset Boulevard: America As Brought to You by the People Who Make Television* (New York: Basic Books, 1979).

the very needs of an economy stifled by military expenditure and by bureaucracy and intrinsic inefficiency now seem to favor processes which might mitigate the existing opposition and make it easier to begin a fruitful dialogue and genuine collaboration for peace. (22)

This passage seems to allude to recent pressures within the USSR, articulated by General Secretary Gorbachev, where the military budget consumes nearly 20 percent of the GNP. In the West, the defense budget of the United States has declined relative to GNP and to the federal budget since 1960. In 1988, it stands at 6.1 percent.[49] The pope repeats Paul VI's appeal "that the resources and investments devoted to arms production ought to be used to alleviate the misery of impoverished peoples" (23). The infusion of new moneys might not accomplish that, however, since, as the pope suggests elsewhere, investments in foreign aid are often used corruptly and are often squandered. Certain sorts of systems strangle development. Aid passed through such systems may not reach the impoverished at all.

John Paul II does make one distinction between the faults of the West and the East. He suggests that "the West gives the impression of abandoning itself to forms of growing and selfish isolation." By contrast, "the East in its turn seems to ignore for questionable reasons its duty to cooperate in the task of alleviating human misery" (23). Is this brief criticism of faults adequate to reality?

The pope describes *"the millions of refugees"* as one of the "consequences" of this division in the world, and as "the festering of a *wound*" (24). He knows as well as we do that the direction in which the refugees stream is one way.

The three passages on the "two blocs" in part V occur in the section on "structures of sin" (36). In the East bloc, the very concept of personal sin (the source of all structural sin) is denied. In the West, this concept is the foundation of the social system. Sin is the reason for limited government, with divided powers; for an economy of private initiative and its diversity; and for re-

---

49. The CIA long estimated Soviet defense spending at 14 percent of GNP; in 1988 these estimates had to be revised to 20 percent, after the Soviets admitted their economy had grown at a much lower rate than earlier assumed.

ligious liberty and liberty of conscience, in open pluralism. In the light of his analysis of sin, the pope asserts that in "certain forms of modern 'imperialism' . . . hidden behind certain decisions, apparently inspired only by economics or politics, are real forms of idolatry: of money, ideology, class, technology" (37). There are comparable observations in the mainstream of Western literature, in which Francis Bacon's "idols of thought" is a traditional theme. Such classical writers as Madison in politics and Smith in economics make this theme the foundation of their thinking. Democratic and capitalist institutions are rooted in recognition of this capacity for self-delusion. That is why checks and balances are necessary.

On the surface, these nine passages have boosted in the world press the moral standing of the East, and lowered that of the West; to that extent, their net effect upon the world does not promote the moral theology that is the pope's ultimate aim. Some critics in response have blamed the press. It is true that a close reading of the text does not support the exaggerated focus of the early reports from Rome. Yet those stories did focus, as journalists are trained to do, upon the new encyclical's most surprising and sensational lines.

When one reviews Pope John Paul II's papal utterances as a whole—his frequent praise of United States institutions, for example[50]—and when one reviews the underlying moral theology of this encyclical, even the most exposed lines of his argument are more cautious than first reports suggested.

However, a system constituted by democracy, by the exercise

50. In his first speech upon arriving in the U.S., Pope John Paul II declared: "I come to join you as you celebrate the bicentennial of that great document, the Constitution of the United States of America. I willingly join you in your prayer of thanksgiving to God for the providential way in which the Constitution has served the people of this nation for two centuries: for the union it has formed, the justice it has established, the tranquillity and peace it has ensured, the general welfare it has promoted and the blessings of liberty it has secured.

"I join you also in asking God to inspire you—as Americans who have received so much in freedom and prosperity and human enrichment—to continue to share all this with so many brothers and sisters throughout the other countries of the world who are still waiting and hoping to live according to the standards worthy of the children of God" (*Origins*, 24 September 1987, p. 231).

of private initiative in economics, and by religious liberty, is *intended* for relentless criticism. That is the principle of its development. A lively mind is the cause, not only of economic wealth, but of human progress in all dimensions. Pope John Paul II has said that the main theme of his papacy is "the primacy of the human spirit." That theme animates this encyclical.

Conclusion: The Liberal Society

Pope John Paul II is both more pessimistic and more inspired by human possibilities for creativity than was Pope Paul VI. Both of them failed to study the "economic miracles" of the two decades before they wrote—Paul VI the "European miracle" of 1945-1967, and Pope John Paul II the "East Asian miracle" of 1967-1987. But John Paul II's emphasis on *"the right of economic initiative"* comes closest to explaining the cause of these miracles. Both popes, rather inexplicably, failed to study thoroughly the causes of success stories.

Pope Paul VI underemphasized the internal capacities for creativity in the poor countries, several of which were to astonish the world with their growth after 1967. And in asking the wealthy nations to share their "superfluous" wealth,[51] Paul VI seemed to beg several crucial questions. Will such shared wealth be used for corrupt purposes, in fruitless ways, and in systems whose internal design is bound to strangle development in its crib? Or will there be systematic internal reforms? John Paul II pays significantly greater attention to these questions, but with far less sharpness of detail than current knowledge warrants.

He also goes beyond Paul VI in five vital ways: in his emphasis on *democracy* as an essential condition for authentic development; in his emphasis on *"the right of economic initiative,"* as an essential condition both for meeting the common good, and for respecting the creative subjectivity of the person; and in his em-

---

51. "The superfluous wealth of rich countries should be placed at the service of poor nations. The rule which up to now held good for the benefit of those nearest to us, must today be applied to all the needy of this world. Besides, the rich will be the first to benefit as a result" (*Populorum Progressio*, 49).

phasis upon *religious liberty*, the deprivation of which, he says,
is a deprivation worse than material poverty. Fourth, his declaration that Catholic social teaching does not offer a "third way"
clarifies a long-standing misconception. His stress on freedom
as the "fundamental category" and "first principle of action" for
Catholic social teaching adds to "justice" and "peace" the value
indispensable to a freely given faith, *ordered liberty*.

Under Pope John Paul II, Catholic social thought is steadily
advancing. Not only did Cardinal Ratzinger's two letters on liberation theology, particularly the second, make available to the
Church a usable definition of Christian "liberty."[52] But here in
Sollicitudo Rei Socialis, John Paul II speaks of "freedom" as a
"fundamental category" and "the first principle of action."
Whether one regards the political order, the economic order, or
the cultural order—the three orders mirrored in the structure of
Vatican II's *Gaudium et Spes*—Pope John Paul II comes down on
the side of ordered liberty. He stands, fundamentally, as what
Americans would call a "liberal," in at least three ways.

Regarding the political order, John Paul asserts that democracy,
the rule of law, limited government, and respect for human
rights are "essential conditions" of a social order conformable
to God's will.

---

52. See "Instruction on Certain Aspects of the 'Theology of Liberation,'" *Origins*, 13 September 1984; "Instruction on Christian Freedom and
Liberation" (Vatican City: Vatican Polyglot Press, 1986). The latter Instruction provides a careful description of Christian liberty (sec. 73): "The supreme commandment of love leads to the full recognition of the dignity
of each individual, created in God's image. From this dignity flow natural rights and duties. In the light of the image of God, freedom, which is
the essential prerogative of the human person, is manifested in all its
depth. Persons are the active and responsible objects of social life.

"Intimately linked to the *foundation,* which is man's dignity, are the
principle of solidarity and the *principle of subsidiarity.*

"By virtue of the first, man with his brothers is obliged to contribute
to the common good of society at all its levels. Hence the Church's doctrine is opposed to all the forms of social or political individualism.

"By virtue of the second, neither the State nor any society must ever
substitute itself for the initiative and responsibility of individuals and of
intermediate communities at the level on which they can function, nor
must they take away the room necessary for their freedom. Hence the
Church's social doctrine is opposed to all forms of collectivism" (emphasis in original).

Regarding the economic order, the pope emphasizes in a new way that *"the right of economic initiative"* is the fundamental principle of authentic development. This right springs from the image of God that inspires human subjectivity. Through it, humans are endowed by God with an inalienable creativity, which serves the common good of all. By the same token, all of creation is destined for the common good of all. Experience has shown that regimes of private property and private initiative better develop the resources of nature than do collectivist or traditionalist regimes, both of which are statist in different ways and degrees.[53] As a limitation on the power of the state, the right to private initiative is necessary both for personal creativity and for the common good.

Regarding the moral order, the pope makes religious freedom, pluralism, and the transcendent rights of conscience central to authentic development. The deprivation of such rights is worse than material deprivation. He says no scheme of development can justify imposing one's own faith or religion upon others.

Where these moral criteria of John Paul II are given expression in the institutions of society, such a society would properly be called a "free society" in the honorific sense.

---

53. The distinguishing characteristic of a capitalist system is neither private property nor markets nor profit, since all these also appear in pre-capitalist, traditionalist systems (cf. Jerusalem in the biblical era). What a capitalist system adds to traditionalist systems is a social system organized to promote *the creativity of the human mind.* Precisely defined, capitalism is the mind-centered system of universal opportunity. Among the institutions supporting the creativity of the mind are: a system of risk and private initiative; a system of personal choice and personal incentives; copyright and patent laws "to promote the progress of science and useful arts"; universal education; institutes of higher education and research, such as are embodied in the U.S. Land Grant College Act of 1862; popular institutions making credit available to the poor and the underprivileged; open access to markets through cheap and swift legal incorporation of new businesses; and social reinforcement for a new moral virtue (which in many languages lacks even a proper name), *enterprise* or *personal initiative.* Enterprise is the habit of attentiveness and alertness to new and improved ways of doing or making. (See Israel M. Kirzner, *Discovery and the Capitalist Process* [Chicago: University of Chicago Press, 1985]; and Michael Novak, *Will It Liberate? Questions About Liberation Theology* [Mahwah, New Jersey: Paulist Press, 1986], chap. 10, "The Constitution of Liberty.")

Thus, despite the clear signs of being the work of a committee; of having been delayed by internal disputes; of displaying sudden insertions and unexplained turns in the argument; of diverse literary styles; and of an organization anything but tightly logical, *Sollicitudo Rei Socialis* does succeed in advancing Catholic social teaching beyond Paul VI in *Populorum Progressio*, and even beyond *Laborem Exercens*. As an inquiry into "the nature and characteristics of authentic human development," it blazes a rough trail for the future. Later inquiries will no doubt sharpen and deepen its principles yet further and organize them more tightly. At some point, too, papal documents will draw lessons from "success stories," since all the world wishes to learn how to build successful institutions of political liberty, economic creativity, and cultural vitality.

It is not easy being the pontiff ("bridge") of a universal Church. Factions within the Church view reality in many quite different horizons. Such factions, pitted against one another in civil argument and in due regard for the lessons of experience, can spur each other to achieve the ultimate good of all. The competition of ideas is as necessary to Catholic social thought as it is to the free society. Those who value the liberal society may rejoice that so many central liberal ideals are slowly gaining acceptance, one by one, in the Church's continuing reflection.

Finally, it would be a real challenge for the Church to conduct an inquiry into the specific economic failures of Catholic nations around the world, such as those of Latin America and, among its successful Confucian neighbors, the Philippines. Are there important gaps in Catholic thought and traditions? Why do some Catholic nations develop so slowly? Why are Catholic peoples so much more vulnerable than Protestants to Communist parties?[54] It would be a real challenge for the Church,

---

54. What, James Billington asks, "is the crucial difference between En gland, America, and Switzerland, where revolutionary traditions did not develop, and France, Italy, and Poland (as well as other Slavic, Germanic, and Latin lands), where they did?

"England, America, and Switzerland . . . had previously experienced and *legitimized ideological opposition* to medieval Catholicism. They were, in short, nations in which Protestantism was, if not the dominant creed as in America, at least a venerable and coequal one as in Switzerland. Secondly, each of these nations in different ways had found ways to institu-

during the next decade or so, to concentrate specifically upon
economic development in Catholic nations. This would test
Catholic methods against alternate methods. It would also fulfill the maxim: Charity begins at home. Were Catholic nations
quickly to become world leaders in human development—and
in invention in every dimension—the credibility of Catholic social thought would be much enhanced.

---

tionalize political opposition through an effective system of parties." Billington adds: "Much experience in nineteenth-century Europe supports
the argument that Protestantism and parliamentarianism provided a kind
of alternative equivalent to revolution" (*Fire in the Minds of Men: Origins
of the Revolutionary Faith* [New York: Basic Books, 1980], pp. 203-04).

Empirical Testings

PETER L. BERGER

It is clear that a papal encyclical must be understood in terms of a very complex ecclesial, political, and theological context. Experts in these matters will be alert to every nuance, every departure (however slight) from previous papal pronouncements, every Catholic and non-Catholic interest that had to be taken into account. I am not one of these experts and I must leave this kind of contextual exegesis to those who are. Yet this encyclical, like others before it, is explicitly addressed to a much wider audience—*urbi et orbi*, as it were—and it purports to give moral guidance to men of good will, Catholic as well as non-Catholic, with a concern for the issues it addresses. As a non-Catholic with a long-standing concern, professional as well as personal, for these issues, I can only comment on this document as it stands on its own and as if it were written by anyone seeking to instruct me in this area. Specifically, I will deal with its empirical assumptions and with its probable empirical consequences, and in conclusion I will try to raise some questions about the usefulness to such as myself of this type of statement.

Looking at the document in this way, I regret to say, has been for me a depressing exercise. It raises one very useful issue. It balances this with one very unfortunate point. Most of it says things that are hard to disagree with, but which are so general and abstract that one is at a loss how to apply what is said here to any concrete social problem. And this last characteristic creates (in my case, reinforces) doubt about the practical utility

110

of the much-vaunted Catholic social doctrine of which this encyclical is a rather typical expression.

If there is one theme that permeates the document, it is that
development means more than economic progress. True development, it insists, must be an improvement of the human condition in all its aspects, including the amplification of human
rights and of freedom, and last not least the protection of man's
transcendent and spiritual nature. In this, the document not only
follows in the footsteps of *Populorum Progressio*, whose twentieth
anniversary it celebrates, but it also conforms to what has been
a growing consensus among secular students of development
for about as long a time. Since the mid-seventies, at least, there
have been few proponents of the earlier "developmentalism"
(*desarrollismo*, as it was called in Latin America) or "growthman-
ship" which equated development with a steady increase in the
gross national product. I fully agree with this near-consensus,
and it is certainly gratifying to see that the pope agrees too, but
there is nothing new to be learned here.

The section of the encyclical that most lends itself to empirical analysis is, of course, the one entitled "Survey of the Contemporary World" (though several themes from this are taken
up again in later sections). It contains a mix of empirically sup-
portable and empirically questionable assumptions.

On the empirical side, the document proposes that differences in culture and value systems can be relevant to development, thus endorsing a valid point that is still often overlooked
by development analysts (especially by economists on the Right
and all sorts of neo-Marxists on the Left). There is the statement
that totalitarianism (so named, contrary to Left prejudices) is an
obstacle to development, understood in the aforementioned
amplified sense, and that the violation of human rights should
be the imposition of another "form of poverty." Again here the
underlying theme is that development is more than economic
growth, as conversely poverty is more than economic deprivation. The designation of the debt crisis as an obstacle to development in many countries is empirically unobjectionable, as is
the observation that international financial arrangements often
work in counterproductive ways. While the overall tone of the
argument is pessimistic, there is mention of the fact that there
have been signs of progress in some developing countries. These

countries are not named. If they were, it would turn out that most of them are in Eastern Asia, and further elaboration of this would have raised questions about the reasons for these countries' success—questions that would have led to invidious comparisons that might have been embarassing in this context.

Rejecting Egalitarianism

The most useful issue raised in this section (it is brought up again later) has to do with what is called here *"the right of economic initiative."* The document affirms this "right," deplores its suppression in the name of a falsely understood ideal of equality, and relates it to the broader moral goal of enhancing *"the creative subjectivity of the citizen"* (15). The way in which these points are made is cautious, and the implications are not spelled out. However, as far as my knowledge goes, this is the first time that a papal encyclical has at any rate come close to affirming the value of free enterprise and to linking the latter with the goal of democratic governance. By the same token, there is here a repudiation of economic egalitarianism (the text comes out against "leveling down" [15]) which places the pope, however gingerly, in opposition to many views held by the Catholic Left. The issue here is empirical as well as ideological. The data support the pope's position: Egalitarian policies tend to constrain economic development, and the costs of this constraint are borne above all by the poor.

It would be too much to expect to have a papal encyclical come out for capitalist models of development. What is more, in another part of the same section there is a repudiation of *"liberal capitalism"* (20) that stands in rather blatant contradiction to the endorsement of *"economic initiative."* Still, Catholic social doctrine has always had great difficulties with the market economy and more generally with the question of what makes for productivity. Its focus (for reasons that undoubtedly go back to a persistent medieval imagination) has been on distribution ("distributive justice") rather than on production. A good case can be made that this nonproductive ethic has been a factor in the poor economic performance of a number of Catholic countries, especially those coming out of the tradition of Iberian

Catholicism. This is why this point made here, however quietly, is to be welcomed.

On the minus side, speaking empirically, the document takes what is probably an overly pessimistic view of the Third World. It speaks of "deterioration" (16), which is clearly true of some parts of the world (notably sub-Saharan Africa). It also asserts that the gap between developed and developing societies has been widening. This notion of the widening gap is a core proposition of Third World ideology. It is questionable. Although the data are not conclusive, at least parts of the Third World have been growing more rapidly than the advanced industrial societies. The discussion of housing and employment problems in the First World is unpersuasive. It is not clear at all that the *"sources of work"* are shrinking (18). While unemployment is always a problem in a modern economy (and, incidentally, not only a capitalist one—socialist economies simply disguise it), a more plausible statement is that patterns of work have been shifting rather than shrinking, though it remains correct that this too entails dislocations and suffering (for example, ask any American steel worker about this). Further, the document reiterates another conventional view of the Left, to the effect that the arms race prevents the allocation of resources to socially useful programs. The arms race may be deplored for any number of moral reasons, but this is very likely not a valid one. In a cold economic logic, defense-related production has generated employment, technological innovation (some of it of great social utility, as in the fallout of space technology for medicine), and higher standards of living.

Tercermundismo

The most unfortunate point made in the document (the one, of course, that was promptly picked up in the first press reports) is in the discussion of the *"two opposing blocs."* In addition to being a threat to peace, the "logic of blocs" is supposed to be a major obstacle to development (20). This in itself is empirically doubtful. On the contrary, one could make the argument that, precisely because of the rivalry between the two "blocs," rich countries have been induced to assist poor ones and to concern themselves

with situations of Third World poverty to which they might
otherwise have remained indifferent. (Should one remind a pope
that God sometimes works through the Assyrians?)

But more importantly unfortunate is the even-handed and
thoroughly misleading treatment of the two blocs. Two systems,
designated as *"liberal capitalism"* and *"Marxist collectivism,"* con-
front each other all over the world. Both are "imperfect and in
need of radical correction." Both are imperialist and neo-
colonialist (21-22). The nature of the respective "imperfections"
is specified further on in the encyclical. Here the assertion is
made that the Church must be critical of both systems, and their
respective ideologies, because the Church must question
whether either can promote "a true and integral development"
(21).

This, of course, is pure Third Worldism *(tercermundismo)*. The
language here is that of such Third World fora as UNCTAD or
UNIDO. There are various points that one can question empirically: Can one really speak here of two ideologies? (Marxism
certainly is, but is "liberal capitalism"?) Is the *"imperialism"* of
the Soviet Union really comparable with whatever one may call
today the *"imperialism"* of the West? And is the word "imperfections" the *mot juste* when one thinks of, among other things, the
Gulag? But within the argument of the encyclical this even-
handed treatment of East and West (in so many words, an ele-
gant version of a "plague-on-both-your-houses" neutralism) is
in sharp contradiction to everything the pope says here about
(precisely) "true and integral development." Of course no existing social system is ever "perfect." But, given the empirical
realities of the contemporary world, which of the two rival systems comes closer to realizing the human values so fervently affirmed in this encyclical? The respect for human rights? Freedom? The protection of spiritual values? It seems to me that even
the most cursory empirical inquiry can answer these questions
without too much difficulty (and, incidentally, without doing so
in an uncritical celebration of the West). It also seems to me that
this pope should have very little difficulty in this comparison. I
must leave it to the Vaticanologists to speculate as to why,
nevertheless, he chooses here to take a neutral position between
Eastern totalitarianism and the democratic capitalism of the
West. The fact that he does is the most negative feature of the

entire document and ipso facto undermines the moral authority as well as the empirical plausibility of this encyclical.

The main themes of this *tour d'orizon* of the contemporary world surface again in subsequent sections of the document, with some additional elaborations. In the section on "Authentic Human Development," underdevelopment is compared with "*superdevelopment*," an alleged First World malady in which there is an overabundance of material goods, leading to waste, materialism, "consumerism" (28). This, of course, is standard cultural criticism in Western countries; its empirical status is hard to establish: Are people really more materialistic when they have much as against when they have little, and how is one to measure this? In the section on "A Theological Reading of Modern Problems," the two "blocs" are taken up again. This time their respective "imperialisms" are designated as "structures of sin" (I suppose that this constitutes a "theological reading"). And here again there is a fine balance: The sin of the West is supposed to be the "*all-consuming desire for profit*," that of the East the "*thirst for power*" (37). What can one say to *this*, in an "empirical reading"? All economic actors, including those in socialist countries, are after "profit"; and all political actors, including those in Western democracies, are in pursuit of power. The assignment of these two "sins" to the respective systems is simplistic and totally abstract. The empirically useful question is how both economic privilege and political power are organized in the two systems, and to whose benefit. As before, the pope does not address this question. Once again in this section, development is linked to peace: the document approvingly quotes a well-known phrase from *Populorum Progressio*, to the effect that development is "the new name for peace" (39). The point is in sharp contradiction with what has just been said about the two superpowers—both developed, yet hardly at peace with each other. Empirically speaking, I think, one would have to say that the relation between degree of development and international peace is more or less random.

A Spirit of Initiative

In "Some Particular Guidelines" it is emphasized that the

Church cannot offer technical solutions for the problems of society, but rather that the Church has something significant to offer as an "expert in humanity" (41). This rather unhappy phrase also comes from *Populorum Progressio;* it grates on the ears of a non-Catholic (especially given the "expertise" displayed by this document). However, the point is elaborated rather usefully in what follows: it is asserted that the social doctrine of the Church is not a "third way" between the rival systems, but rather constitutes "a category of its own," offering moral critiques of these (and, by implication, any other) socioeconomic system. Thus, when the Church speaks of a *"preference for the poor"* or insists that private property is under a "social mortgage" (that one is a much more felicitous phrase; it has been used by the pope in earlier statements), it is not delineating a socioeconomic blueprint of its own but rather promoting moral principles that others can use in their own designs. This is useful because a number of Catholic thinkers (particularly in Latin America) continue to speak of a "third way" beyond both capitalism and socialism (41-42). The empirical details of this putative "third way" have never been clear and, in my opinion, this rhetoric has served as a way of avoiding the hard choices to be made in the real world. It is good to have the pope repudiate this particular fantasy.

In the same section there is a reiteration of the point that development demands a "spirit of initiative" and that poor countries should discover their *"own area of freedom"* (this presumably means windows of economic opportunity) instead of always looking for favors from the richer countries. This is the most positive statement in the document, now highlighted again, and that is to be welcomed. There is also another condemnation of corrupt and dictatorial regimes, and a call for democratic and participatory government. I would certainly not want to quarrel with this. But then the document asserts that such government is the *"necessary condition and sure guarantee"* of development (44). This is what Jeane Kirkpatrick kept saying at the United Nations. I wish it were so; I don't think it is. Empirically speaking, one may say that capitalism is the necessary condition of democracy (precisely the proposition that this document goes to great lengths to avoid). One may also say, cautiously, that successful capitalist development (and, possibly, relatively

successful socialist development) releases certain democratiz-
ing pressures. Unfortunately, one cannot say that democracy is
the necessary condition of successful development. Some of the
biggest success stories in development have taken place under
dictatorial and nondemocratic political auspices, beginning
with the most important case, that of Meiji, Japan.

In the conclusion of the document the term "liberation" is ap-
propriated to designate human freedom and authenticity in
very general terms. This repeats what was done in earlier Vatican statements about Liberation Theology, affirming its underlying humane impulse while repudiating many of its specifics.
Against any form of social utopianism, the document concludes
that "*no temporal achievement*," however praiseworthy, is to be
identified with the Kingdom of God (48). This relativization of
political and social programs is very much what one would wish
to hear from the Church; I myself would even say that in such
relativization lies a key sociopolitical contribution that the
Church can make to a world prone to fanaticism.

Final Grades

Is this a useful document? Its likely empirical consequences will
be different in different parts of the world. In the West, by and
large, the document will provide comfort and support to the religious Left, to the "peace and justice" crowd who have a high
stake in speaking of East and West in morally equivalent terms
and who perceive the Third World as a victim of profit-thirsty,
power-hungry imperialisms. This is definitely a minus point. In
the East, the pope's home territory, the document is likely to give
further support to those who seek reform within the socialist
system—no doubt a plus point. And in the so-called South the
document's most useful point, the one about economic enterprise, may provide a useful modulation of the prevailing Third
World ideology. On balance, then, the document may do more
good than harm.

That, however, is a *political* assessment, quite independent of
the substance, the empirical validity of what is said here. This
substance, I must repeat, is very thin indeed. As an empirically
tenable and practically useful description of the contemporary

world, I would grade this document somewhere between a C+ and a B-. While this is not so bad, given what the level of intellectual discourse on these matters is today, one must ask whether anything is gained, for Catholics or non-Catholics, by such expressions of what is considered to be an authoritative doctrine about the right ordering of society. I recognize that Rome is impelled to keep on producing such statements by its conception of the magisterium of the Church, a conception that I do not share. But, even given these theological and ecclesial assumptions—that is, looking at this document and indeed at the growing body of Catholic social doctrine from a *Catholic* point of view—I wonder what is gained from these exercises. Very possibly they actually undermine the authority of the teaching mission that they are supposed to express. I'm reminded of the reply given by Samuel Gompers to the question as to what the American labor movement wants: *"More!"* he replied. I ask myself what I would want from Rome in terms of its social doctrine. Respectfully, regretfully, but with increasing assurance I find myself replying: *less!*

The Democracy Connection

GEORGE WEIGEL

Sollicitudo Rei Socialis, like any Roman document of its genre, has to be understood, not simply on its own terms, but in the context of modern papal social teaching, which of course begins with Leo XIII's 1891 encyclical *Rerum Novarum,* "On the Condition of the Working Classes." That English title aptly characterizes the issues which focused papal attention for some seventy years: the questions of economic justice, public order, and secularization which had been posed by the rapid industrialization and modernization of Europe. This definition of "the social question" as having to do primarily with advanced industrial societies continued through Pius XI's 1931 encyclical *Quadragesimo Anno,* but began to shift toward a more explicitly international focus with John XXIII's 1961 *Mater et Magistra:* a shift confirmed by the encyclical which *Sollicitudo Rei Socialis* is intended to commemorate, Paul VI's *Populorum Progressio.* By 1967, in other words, "the Church's social concern" was decisively focused on the circumstances of the world's underclass in the so-called "Third World," a specification given added impetus by the 1971 Synodal document "Justice in the World."

Others in this symposium will address the economic judgments made by these expressions of modern Catholic social thought. Here, I want to locate *Sollicitudo Rei Socialis* within a parallel tradition of papal, conciliar, and synodal teaching, the tradition which I have termed "the Catholic human rights rev-

119

olution."[1] The *locus classicus* for this striking development
(which has seen Roman Catholicism transform itself from a bas-
tion of the *ancien regime* to perhaps the world's most visible institutional defender of human rights) was the Second Vatican
Council's "Declaration on Religious Freedom," *Dignitatis Humanae Personae*, whose Latin title encapsulated the personalist
philosophical approach which undergirded the Church's defense of the primary human right of religious freedom or freedom of conscience.

John Paul II has both extended and transformed modern
Catholic social teaching on human rights through his own encyclicals, his addresses to various diplomatic representatives to
the Holy See, and his sermons and addresses during his extensive pastoral travels. To be drastically brief, what the present
pope has done is add explicitly political-structural concerns to
the philosophical personalism of *Dignitatis Humanae Personae*.
That is, the pope has raised, on numerous occasions, the question of what political models for the right ordering of human
society are most congruent with the array of "rights" which the
Church deems essential to "integral human development." The
implications of this politicization (in the best sense of the term)
of Catholic human rights teaching for the pastoral mission of the
Church have become evident in locales as various as Central and
Latin America, the Philippines, and central and eastern Europe.[2]

The Revised Standard Version

Sollicitudo Rei Socialis continues this trend by linking human
rights and democratization to Third World economic development in a striking way. John Paul II says, as popes do and must,
that his work is an extension of the thought of his predecessors.
But on the questions of human rights and democracy, it is an extension by way of a sharp differentiation.

---

1. Cf. my essay "John Courtney Murray and the Catholic Human
Rights Revolution," *This World* 15 (Summer 1987): pp. 14-27.
2. For a more detailed analysis of this development, cf. my essay "Religious Freedom: The First Human Right," *This World* 21 (Spring 1988): pp.
31-45.

Whereas *Populorum Progressio* was virtually silent on the question of the relationship between different political regimes and the prospects for economic development, *Sollicitudo Rei Socialis* makes no bones about the kinds of polities it deems most likely to contribute to economic development narrowly construed, and to "integral human development" in the fullest sense of the term. Whereas *Populorum Progressio* favored state-centered approaches to development strategy,[3] *Sollicitudo Rei Socialis* teaches that any such state-sponsored efforts must be in the context of what the pope calls the individual's *"right of economic initiative,"* which sounds rather like saying "the right of entrepreneurship." And whereas *Populorum Progressio* seemed to give a tacit papal benediction to the priority of so-called "economic and social rights" over civil rights and political freedoms, which in the activist vulgate became the maxim "bread before freedom," *Sollicitudo Rei Socialis* teaches that bread comes *through* freedom: through the acknowledgment in theory and practice of the equality, indeed one might even argue priority, of civil rights and political freedoms in a society of "solidarity."

There are at least five points at which *Sollicitudo Rei Socialis* should be seen as a conceptual advance beyond the teaching of *Populorum Progressio* on this matter of human rights, democracy, and development.

(1) The first has just been mentioned: the pope's insistence on the *"right of economic initiative."* Its suppression, the pope writes, leads to "passivity, dependence and submission to the bureaucratic apparatus which, as the only 'ordering' and 'decision-making' body—if not also the 'owner'—of the entire totality of goods and the means of production, puts everyone in a position of almost absolute dependence." Nor are the rights of economic initiative and entrepreneurship to be denied on the basis of "an alleged 'equality' of everyone in society," which the pope correctly understands to result in neither social equity nor material prosperity (15).

(2) The encyclical is just as firm in its rejection of totalitarian

---

3. "It is the function of *public authorities* to establish and enjoin the [development] objectives to be obtained, the plans to be followed, and the means to achieve them; also to stimulate the energies of all involved in this common activity" (*Populorum Progressio*, 33 [emphasis added]).

approaches to development. "No social group," the pope writes, ". . . has the right to usurp the role of sole leader, since this brings about the destruction of the true subjectivity of society and of the individual citizens, as happens in every form of totalitarianism." The illustration of a "social group" which has attempted such a hegemonic role is given as "for example a political party," and the referents here seem clear enough: Marxist-Leninist parties and the one-party states of the Third World (15).

(3) The pope sharpens this point even more explicitly a few paragraphs later in the encyclical. Judging that, in the aggregate, things have gotten "*notably worse*" in the developing world, the pope argues that responsibility for this is not unilinear, and cites the "undoubtedly grave instances of omissions on the part of the developing nations themselves, and especially on the part of those holding economic and political power" (16). Inept, brutal, and ideologically hidebound Third World governments are, in other words, held responsible in considerable part for the deterioration of economic conditions in their countries. Responsibility for Third World destitution does not lie exclusively in the developed world. "Development demands above all a spirit of initiative on the part of the countries which need it" (44). Political reform must be part of a morally (and empirically) sound development strategy. These are all themes notable by their absence from *Populorum Progressio*.

(4) Perhaps even more striking is the pope's teaching on the appropriate political models for development. Economic development will not take place absent what we might call a "civil society," or, in John Paul II's own words, "*the developing nations themselves* should favor the *self-affirmation* of each citizen, through access to a wider culture and a free flow of information*" (44). But civil rights in a civil society are not matters of declaration or proclamation alone; as James Madison warned two hundred years ago, rights are not secured by "parchment barriers." In addition to the moral skills of a people, development (in both the wider and narrower senses of the term) requires that Third World countries "reform certain unjust structures, and in particular their *political institutions*, in order to replace corrupt, dictatorial, and authoritarian forms of government by *democratic* and *participatory* ones." The democratic revolution in the Third

World is one that John Paul II hopes "will spread and grow stronger," because "the 'health' of a political community—as expressed in the free and responsible participation of all citizens in public affairs, in the rule of the law and in respect for the promotion of human rights—is the *necessary condition and sure guarantee* of the development of 'the whole individual and of all people'" (44).

(5) This striking papal endorsement of democracy as both morally and pragmatically linked to development is rooted in the encyclical's human rights teaching. John Paul II clearly wants the "development" debate to include more than the question of material standards of living. Poverty in this world has many forms and names, the pope teaches. "The denial or the limitation of human rights—as for example the right to religious freedom, the right to share in the building of society, the freedom to organize and to form unions, or to take initiatives in economic matters—do these not impoverish the human person as much as, if not more than, the deprivation of material goods? And is development which does not take into account the full affirmation of these rights really development on the human level?" The questions, asked, seem to answer themselves, at least in the mind of John Paul II, who sums up these concerns by writing that "modern underdevelopment is not only economic but also cultural, political and simply human" (15).

It cannot be said, therefore, that *Sollicitudo Rei Socialis* simply recapitulates and sharpens the teaching and development approach of *Populorum Progressio*, as commentators who favor the priority of "economic and social rights" over civil rights and political freedoms have argued.[4] On the contrary, and on these five specific and crucial points, John Paul II has taken the papal discussion in a significantly different direction. One can even argue that *Sollicitudo Rei Socialis* is the most forthright defense of the moral imperative of democracy in authoritative Catholic social teaching. In this sense, the encyclical should be read as a papal reconfirmation of the line taken by the 1986 Vatican "Instruction on Christian Freedom and Liberation," which taught that "authentic development" in poor countries requires open

---

4. Cf., for example, Peter Hebblethwaite's analysis in the *National Catholic Reporter*, 26 February 1988, p. 7.

political systems in which there is "a real separation between the powers of the State."[5]

The reasons for this evolution in papal social teaching are worth speculating on, briefly. Certainly the pope's own experience of the stultifying economic and cultural circumstances of many of the countries of central and eastern Europe is one factor in John Paul's preferential option for democracy. *Sollicitudo Rei Socialis* will thus reinforce the critiques mounted in recent years by such central European intellectuals as Vaclav Havel in Czechoslovakia, Georg Konrad in Hungary, and Adam Michnik in Poland. What Havel terms the "culture of the lie" in these societies is clearly, in the mind of John Paul II, an obstacle to integral human development, as well as to material well-being.[6]

The experience of the Church in Central and South America, and in east Asia, would also seem to be a factor here. On the matter of *"the right of economic initiative"* (15), John Paul is almost certainly aware of the efforts of men such as Peru's Hernando de Soto (supported by the novelist and publicist Mario Vargas Llosa) who argue the case against classic Latin American mercantilism and for entrepreneurship as the road to economic development. De Soto's "other path" and John Paul II's teaching on economic initiative would seem to have much in common.[7]

---

5. "Instruction on Christian Freedom and Liberation," 95.

6. For an analysis of the new intellectual ferment in central Europe, cf. Timothy Garton Ash, "Does Central Europe Exist?" *New York Review of Books,* 9 October 1986.

7. De Soto's book *The Other Path,* a title in deliberate contrast to the "shining path" of Peru's Maoist guerillas, is a best-seller throughout Latin America. Its perspective is summarized in this news report:

"In dozens of ways big and small, Mr. de Soto's 'other path' challenges the beliefs that prevail throughout Latin America. To the left, which argues that capitalism has failed in the region, Mr. de Soto responds that 'Latin America has never experienced true modern capitalism.' Similarly, while arguing that the Roman Catholic Church should properly pursue an option for the poor, he questions some tenets of liberation theology. 'Let's not confuse the poor with the unemployed proletariat,' he said in an interview. . . . 'The poor are also entrepreneurs, so don't tell me that the only way I can help them is through Marxist-Leninist means.' But Mr. de Soto is no less critical of the right wing, which he views as an impediment to the emergence of a truly popular capitalism. 'They distrust the idea of being controlled by all these little copper-colored people,' he said. He is

Nor can the failures of the Nicaraguan revolution—in terms of civil rights, political freedoms, and material well-being—have escaped the attention of a pope who was, after all, shouted down by Sandinista leaders during a Mass in Managua in March 1983. John Paul's roots lead some commentators to think that the Polish prism is the only optic through which the pope reads world politics and economics. No doubt the pope has a special concern for conditions in his native land. But the extensive nature of the pope's travels in Latin America ought not be discounted. John Paul II knows that a fragile democratic revolution is underway in Latin America, and it seems clear that he wants to position the Church on its side, as against either traditional authoritarianisms or the siren-songs of Marxism-Leninism. The same could, of course, be said about the pope's perception of the present realities in the Philippines and South Korea.

The Problem of "Moral Equivalence"

That these themes—the "bread *through* freedom" themes—in *Sollicitudo Rei Socialis* have not framed the debate over the encyclical has at least something to do with the bias in favor of "economic and social rights" that one finds throughout the American Catholic intellectual, journalistic, and activist elite.[8] But the game of "spin-control" (as they call it in Washington) aside, it has to be acknowledged that the encyclical itself creates major hermeneutic difficulties by its analysis of the East/West "bloc" system and its impact on the Third World.

The themes in question are familiar enough and can be

---

critical of regimes such as that of Gen. Augusto Pinochet of Chile, arguing that 'what is crucial for any government to adapt itself to the emerging market is democracy'" (*New York Times*, 27 December 1987).

8. The National Catholic News Service's "at-a-glance" summary of the encyclical failed to mention even one of the themes sketched above, while NC's longer sidebar said nothing about the pope's endorsement of democracy. (Printed in *The Progress*, newspaper of the Archdiocese of Seattle, 25 February 1988, pp. 10-11).

The most notable exception to this pattern in the general press was Peter Steinfels's able commentary on the encyclical in the *New York Times*, 20 February 1988.

rapidly summarized. Both East and West, "Marxist collectivism" and "liberal capitalism," are "imperfect and in need of
radical correction." Their rivalry, transferred to the Third World,
is a "direct obstacle to the real transformation of the conditions
of underdevelopment in the developing and less advanced
countries." Moreover, "each of the two *blocs* harbors in its own
way a tendency toward *imperialism,* as it is usually called, or
towards forms of new-colonialism." Each is further marked by
"an unacceptably exaggerated concern *for security,* which deadens the impulse towards united cooperation by all for the common good of the human race" (21, 22).

These themes were criticized, at various levels of dudgeon,
by several prominent commentators. William Safire was first
out of the rhetorical blocks, arguing that "Pope John Paul II
risks becoming known as the foremost moral-political relativist of our times."[9] William F. Buckley, Jr., characterized the
pope's geopolitics as "this Tweedledum-Tweedledee view of
the crystallized division between the visions of Marx, Lenin,
Mao Tse-tung, and Pol Pot over against those of Locke, Jefferson, Lincoln and Churchill," and urged that "the Holy Father
. . . move quickly to correct an encyclical heart-tearingly mis-
begotten."[10] And, several ideological notches *à gauche,* the
editors of the *New Republic* claimed that the pope had "become an apostle of moral equivalence" who had failed "to tell
the whole truth" at least in part because of "political considerations."[11]

About all of which, several points are in order.

First, it must be said (and especially to those inclined to support his moral leadership in world politics) that John Paul II is
not, cannot, and should not be the chaplain of the Western alliance. His is a universal ministry to a universal Church. This is
ecclesiological bedrock, and ought to be understood as such.
Moreover, one can make the case, and strictly in terms of the war
of ideas in world politics, that it in fact serves the purpose of

---

9. William Safire, "Structures of Sin," *New York Times,* 22 February 1988,
p. A-19.
10. William F. Buckley, Jr., "What is the Pope Saying?" *National Review,*
18 March 1988, pp. 17-18.
11. "Papal Gull," *New Republic,* 14 March 1988, pp. 5-7.

human rights and democracy for the pope to press these causes from a position self-consciously ahead of today's international divisions.

Second, the themes of *Sollicitudo Rei Socialis* which clearly distinguish it from earlier papal documents on development are precisely those themes which are most critical, implicitly *and explicitly*, of Marxist-Leninist development schemes. The pope's teaching on the right of economic initiative, his rejection of statist approaches to development, and his linkage between human rights and development, and democracy and development, are going to read quite differently in Moscow, Havana, and Managua than in New York and Washington. The denizens of the former locales will know full well who is in the moral dock on these points. The denizens of the latter locales should do what they can to raise up that point.

Third, one has to bear in mind the pope's concerns for central Europe in general and Poland in particular. To say, in Poland, that one wishes freedom from the "bloc" system is to say that one wants to be free from the control of that power which uses the "bloc" imagery to buttress, ideologically and rhetorically, its hegemonic purposes. Which is to say, criticism of the "bloc" system in the Polish context is criticism of the Soviet Union, and is understood to be such by both Poles and Soviets.

Finally, *Sollicitudo Rei Socialis* must be interpreted within the context of John Paul II's entire corpus of teaching on matters political. Consider, in this respect, the pope's formal remarks to President Reagan in Miami in September 1987:

> Among the many admirable values of [the United States] there is one that stands out in particular. It is freedom. The concept of freedom is part of the very fabric of this nation as a political community of free people. Freedom is a great gift, a blessing of God.
>
> From the beginning of America, freedom was directed to forming a well-ordered society and to promoting its peaceful life. Freedom was channeled to the fullness of human life, to the preservation of human dignity, and to the safeguarding of all human rights. An experience of ordered freedom is truly part of the history of this land.
>
> This is the freedom that America is called upon to live and guard and to transmit. She is called to exercise it in such a way

that it will also benefit the cause of freedom in other nations and among other peoples.[12]

When John Paul II says these same things in Managua, Havana, or Moscow about the regimes in power in those capitals—then, and not until then, will the charge of "moral relativist" stick.

All of that being said, and meant, there are important points in the Safire, Buckley, and *New Republic* criticisms that the Vatican simply must take seriously.

The encyclical is crafted in such a way that it can plausibly (if, in my view, fallaciously) be interpreted as pronouncing a plague on the houses of both "East" and "West." This is not only unfortunate in the domestic United States context (i.e., in terms of the forces, political and ecclesiastical, to which it will give aid and comfort). It is also precisely the wrong signal to send into Central America just now, since it will tend to reinforce the spurious claims of the Sandinistas to "non-aligned status." The Nicaraguan FSLN is no more "non-aligned" than many other members of the Non-Aligned Movement; the pope's description of the latter as an instrument "beyond" ideological geopolitics is, with all respect, simply mistaken.

The pope also confuses the international debate by attributing "neo-colonialist" and "imperialist" tendencies indiscriminately to both "East" and "West." Yes, and viewed from a rather high level of abstraction, each of the world's two great powers "tends to assimilate or gather around it other countries or groups of countries, to different degrees of adherence or participation" (20). But it is precisely the "different degrees of adherence or participation" that define the relevant moral distinctions between the alliances in question. NATO is a defensive alliance comprised of democratic states which have freely chosen to work together for their mutual security—an alliance "gathered" by such eminent democrats as Dean Acheson, Konrad Adenauer, and Ernest Bevin. Moreover, is "gather around it" an accurate description of the way in which Stalin expanded the Soviet empire's sphere of influence in 1944-48? Can one truly compare the "adherence" of countries like, say, France or Spain

---

12. From *Origins* 17, no. 15 (25 September 1987).

to NATO with the "adherence" of East Germany and Czechoslovakia to the Warsaw Pact—an "alliance" held together by the
omnipresence of the Red Army? Historical, empirical, *and moral*
discriminations are surely in order here.

Nor do the relative contributions of "East" and "West" to development assistance in the Third World support the encyclical's seeming charge that both "blocs" are equally deficient in
meeting their responsibilities to the world's underclass. The
Soviet Union and its allies are notorious for their parsimony in
development aid—save in military hardware and training for
repressive "state security" forces. One can argue that the "West"
should do more by way of funding Third World development
projects, but even here the Vatican ought to acknowledge
forthrightly that, on the presently available empirical evidence,
there is no direct and unambiguous correlation between levels
of development aid and actual economic progress. *Sollicitudo Rei
Socialis* does in fact broach this point, in its stress on the responsibilities of Third World countries for initiatives on their own behalf. But that teaching is muted, perhaps to the point of not being
heard, by the encyclical's seemingly even-handed critique of the
development assistance of the "blocs."

It should certainly be possible for the Vatican to stand
"ahead" of the world's geopolitical divisions and still acknowledge these truths. Vatican officials may argue that *Sollicitudo Rei Socialis* is a complex document whose exegesis must
involve a careful reading between the lines, as it were. And
there is something to that argument. On the other hand, the
Vatican (like the rest of us) is living in a media environment
which is notably resistant to complex analyses and subtle
nuances. That may be a shame, but shame or not, it is a fact of
modern life. Thus it can be argued that the Vatican has a moral
and pastoral responsibility to craft documents in such a way
that the lead paragraphs in the next day's *New York Times* read
something other than "Pope John Paul II . . . issued an encyclical letter charging that the ideological rivalry between East
and West was subjecting poor nations to 'structures of sin' that
deny them freedom and development. . . . [The encyclical's]
harshest attack on the superpowers accuses them of playing
out their competition in the third world and thus reducing
developing nations to 'parts of a machine, cogs on a gigantic

wheel.' "[13] I believe that that is a tendentious reading of *Solli-citudo Rei Socialis*, and one which fails to take account of what is truly new and distinctive in the encyclical. But it is, in truth, a plausible summary, given the structure and language of the letter itself.

A classic maxim of Thomistic epistemology should be re-called here: *Quidquid recipitur ad modum recipientis recipitur* ("What is received is received according to the mode of the re-ceiver"). Put more simply, in order to be heard accurately, one has to take account of the prejudices, limitations, and interests of those to whom one is speaking. Put even more simply, people tend to hear what they want to hear. It is hardly a secret that the prestige press in the United States "hears" phrases like "the blocs" and translates these, without further hermeneutic fuss-and-bother, into its own preferred categories of "the superpowers" and their "moral equivalents." If, as I think is demonstrably true from his full corpus of social teaching, John Paul II believes that Marxist-Leninist totalitarianism is a mor-tal threat to spiritual, economic, cultural, and political de-velopment throughout the world, and, conversely, that democracy is morally superior as an instrument of integral human development, then a way must be found to make that moral analysis "hearable" given the regnant media filters. That is not an impossible task, and it need not involve a return to the days of the Pacelli/Spellman alliance. There are many Americans, of broad and deep experience in these matters and occupying various points on the ideological spectrum, who would be eager to help the Vatican make its case in terms that do not lend themselves to distortion. Their counsel should be sought. It does not seem to have been in the case of *Sollicitudo Rei Socialis*.

The Next Phase of Argument

Official Catholicism's historical discomforts with liberal polities and market-oriented economies are well known, and need not

---

13. Roberto Suro, "Papal Encyclical Says Superpowers Hurt Third World," *New York Times*, 20 February 1988, p. 1.

be rehearsed here.[14] Precisely in the light of that history, one might argue that *Sollicitudo Rei Socialis* is, potentially, a fork in the road for Catholic social thought.

That there is a tension in the encyclical between its geopolitical and (in some respects) economic analysis, and its political theory on the matter of human rights and democracy, is obvious. That tension is not resolved by appeals to a supposed higher viewpoint of moral theology, because in a Catholic incarnational context, moral theology is not conducted in a Kantian ether, but rather grapples with this-worldly institutions and practices. The tension, from one angle of vision, is between those parts of *Sollicitudo Rei Socialis* which reach back to *Populorum Progressio* for their inspiration, and those which seem to extend and specify John Paul II's teaching on human rights and democracy.

There is a danger of selective hermeneutics here, and it should be frankly conceded. On the other hand, if one takes seriously the pope's definition of the right of economic initiative, his distaste for statist development strategies, his linkage of development to civil rights and political freedoms, and above all his forthright moral endorsement of democracy, then one can see in *Sollicitudo Rei Socialis* the first glimpses of a new trend in papal social teaching. One can even imagine, *and on the basis of this encyclical*, a new argument evolving within the Church's magisterium, one which takes seriously Peter Berger's hypothesis that "Capitalism is a necessary but not sufficient condition of democracy under modern conditions."[15] Berger's own thoughts on this question might well be thoughts in the mind of John Paul II:

As to the falsification of [this] hypothesis, the most convincing one would be the emergence, in empirical reality rather than in the realm of ideas, of even one clear case of democratic socialism. That such a society will emerge in the future is, of course, the fondest wish of democratic socialists. The future is always open, and social science is not capable of making defini-

---

14. Cf. Michael Novak, *Freedom with Justice: Catholic Social Thought and Liberal Institutions* (San Francisco: Harper & Row, 1984) for a thoughtful overview of the argument since the mid-nineteenth century.

15. Peter L. Berger, *The Capitalist Revolution: Fifty Propositions About Prosperity, Equality, and Liberty* (New York: Basic Books, 1986), p. 81.

tive statements about it. [But] . . . the future emergence of a
democratic socialism is very improbable. . . .

The experience of Western societies would seem to indicate
that a greater degree of political intervention [in the economy]
is possible, with democracy remaining intact, than some pro-
capitalist theorists have thought (including perhaps Hayek).
The resistance to the introduction of market mechanisms in socialist societies by the party and bureaucratic elites also suggests that there is a tilting point in the reverse direction. In
other words, all those apparatchiks have very good grounds
for worrying that, if a socialist system is modified beyond a
certain point by market mechanisms, the new entrepreneurs
will become uppity and start demanding political liberties that
would undermine the control of the party.[16]

John Paul II, with his intense interest in the affairs of central
and eastern Europe and the Soviet Union, his expressed desire
to visit the Peoples Republic of China, and his experience of the
democratic revolution in many parts of the Third World, cannot
be unaware that there is an argument to be engaged at precisely
this point of linkage between market-oriented economies and
the pope's concern for human rights and democracy. The argument is being posed, not just by what would seem to be important trajectories in John Paul II's own social thought, but also by
historical reality: by the development success stories of east
Asia, by the post-Maoist economics of the PRC, by the emergence of fragile democracies in Latin America, the Philippines,
and South Korea, by the struggle over *glasnost* and *perestroika* in
the Soviet Union, and by the cultural, political, and economic
churnings of the Western world. The question, in a sense, is not
whether there is a fork in the road for Catholic social thought,
but whether the fork will be seen for what it is.

There are, to be sure, currents of thought in *Sollicitudo Rei Socialis* which would seem to preclude a careful exploration of the
linkage between human rights, democracy, and capitalist forms
of development. But, as has been argued here at length, there is
enough material in the encyclical to at least open the discussion,
and in a way that takes the empirical realities of development
successes and failures into account.

---

16. Berger, *The Capitalist Revolution*, pp. 81-82.

That the teaching authority of the Catholic Church has given its moral blessing to democracy as the most appropriate political model for integral human development is no small fact. It remains to be seen whether the full implications of that fact are drawn out, and precisely by that same teaching authority.

Sollicitudo Behind the Headlines

RICHARD JOHN NEUHAUS

When trying to untie a knot one looks first for the ends. You pull at them, looking for some give, but gingerly, lest you further tighten the knot. It definitely gets harder if you discover that there are not two, but three or four or more ends. Then you know you have a bunch of strings that can only be disentangled, if at all, with considerable care. *Sollicitudo Rei Socialis* is a tangled document that contains several strings of reasoning, stated and unstated premises not clearly related, and different, although not necessarily conflicting, ends. In this respect it is dramatically different from John Paul's earlier encyclicals, which are believably the products of a writer sitting down and setting forth his thinking on a given subject. At a number of points, *Sollicitudo* has the markings of a committee project and, with due respect, the old aphorism about the horse and the camel does spring to mind.

We should not be surprised. In the introduction the pope offers something of the history of the encyclical's production through the machinery of the Pontifical Commission's *Iustitia et Pax*. And the fact that it was predated almost two months before its actual release suggests that it was held up by last-minute discussions and fine tunings. As of this writing, allegedly "inside" stories are being told about maneuverings relative to the encyclical's production, but those need not concern us here. There is ample evidence internal to the document itself indicating that it had no easy passage from conception to birth.

Given the political polarization within the Church, and in our

134

culture more generally, it is not surprising that people tend to rush to their partisan scoreboards when a papal statement is issued, chalking up how many things he says on "our" side and how many on "theirs." It is more difficult, and much more rewarding, to listen to the argument that is being made, and to keep the different pieces in conversation with one another. Unfortunately—and, again, unlike John Paul's earlier encyclicals—*Sollicitudo* lends itself to scoreboard reading. The communications media are the chief tenders of the cultural and political scoreboard, and they were almost unanimous in the way they scored this encyclical. A. M. Rosenthal of the *New York Times* acknowledged that there are many good and nuanced things said in the letter, but he concludes: "All good journalists would put the same headline on the story: 'Pope Condemns Marxism and Capitalism Equally; Says Both are Imperialistic and Sin Against Poor.'" Even better journalists might have come up with the headline "Pope Says Freedom and Human Rights Essential to Global Development." That headline is at least equally accurate (on balance, I expect it is more accurate), but of course it does not have the pizazz of the first headline's focus on superpower politics. Mr. Rosenthal is right; the headline that *Sollicitudo* received was utterly predictable. For all but those who study the encyclical with some care, that headline has almost entirely eclipsed the argument of the document. Regrettably, this unhappy outcome seems not to have been anticipated in Rome.

It must be admitted that *Sollicitudo* does not have a clear beginning, middle, and end, or at least they are not to be found in their expected places. We might reasonably begin, however, by asking what is the intended purpose of the encyclical, and a good part of the answer is in fact to be found in the beginning of the document. The pope's stated purpose is to continue, under the guidance of the Spirit, the building of the Church's social teaching, so that people will be able to respond with "rational reflection . . . to their vocation as responsible builders of earthly society" (1). Sustaining the continuity of the social teaching also requires renewal through "necessary and opportune adaptations" (3) to changed historical circumstances. A church that is disposed to thinking in terms of centuries, it is suggested, must also be capable of thinking in terms of decades. John Paul

is struck by the rapidity of change in the world since *Populorum
Progressio* and goes so far as to say that "the *configuration of the
world* in the course of the last twenty years, while preserving certain fundamental constants, has undergone notable changes
and presents some totally new aspects" (4).

While most of us might be reluctant to speak of much in the
world that is "totally new," it is worth recalling some of the
changes in the Church and the world since Paul VI issued the
encyclical that the pope is commemorating and developing. In
1967 what came to be called "Liberation Theology" was not a
factor in theology or social action. *Populorum* called for what was
generally understood to be a more socialist direction in politics
and economics without knowing the uses to which that call
might be put. John Paul, on the other hand, is keenly aware of
the distortions of that call. It is noteworthy that in the present
encyclical he no less than eight times invokes the "instructions"
of the Congregation for the Doctrine of the Faith (CDF), with
their rigorous strictures aimed at Liberation Theology. Similarly,
in 1967 Latin American and other Third World Catholics were
not contending that the Church proposes a "third way" between
socialism and capitalism. To be sure, the idea of Catholicism representing a "third way" has been around for half a century or
more, but it has taken on new life in recent years as people try
to steer between Marxist liberationisms and the Vatican's
nineteenth-century understanding of "liberalism." In terms of
Roman Catholic teaching, it is of considerable significance that
John Paul explicitly and firmly rejects the contention that the
Church proposes a "third way" (41). Nor could Paul VI have anticipated subsequent disappointments with the regimes of
former colonies, especially in Africa, that were then newly independent. Nineteen sixty-seven was a time of high hope for the
postcolonial period, and the dashing of so many of those hopes
contributes strongly to John Paul's view that the global situation
has in many respects deteriorated.

In addition, until only a few years ago many people assumed
that socialism, in one form or another, was the wave of the future. Now it is almost universally understood—even in the
former political bastions of socialist ideology such as China and
the Soviet Union—that, while capitalism has produced many
imperfect models of the successful development of formerly

poor countries, socialism has produced no successes at all. Thus John Paul cautions, in a way that Paul VI did not, against a false egalitarianism and central political control that quashes individual initiative and dignity. Finally, upon rereading *Populorum*, one is struck by how much it is a Western document, addressed to Western nations and others within their orbit of influence. *Populorum* mentions "totalitarianism" and societies based on "atheistic" principles, but they are clearly beyond the pale. In John Paul one encounters a man who comes from within that pale. This pope's criticisms of a world locked into "two blocs" must also be understood as a demand for freedom on behalf of his native land and other countries similarly situated in the Soviet *imperium*. It is an understandable instance of ethnocentricism—but nonetheless a serious mistake—for Westerners to interpret *Sollicitudo* in a way that ignores the Pope's concern for how the encyclical will be read in the world from which he comes and to which he is deeply attached.

These, then, are five of the major changes in the "configuration" of the world and the Church since *Populorum*: the emergence of Liberation Theology; the revived currency of the idea that the Church should pioneer a "third way" in the political, social, and economic order; the disappointing, often tragically disappointing, record of postcolonial regimes; the collapse of confidence in the socialist paradigm; and the fuller inclusion of the Eastern bloc in the orbit of papal concern. The last is especially important, I believe, in understanding what many critics of *Sollicitudo* have described as the pope's language of "moral equivalency" between East and West. Some of that language is indeed unfortunate in that it almost invited the misleading headlines that have largely eclipsed the encyclical's message, but a hermeneutics of fairness requires that we understand that language too in relation to the entirety of the encyclical and in relation to John Paul's many other statements on the questions addressed by the encyclical. A hermeneutics of fairness does not require, however, that we deny the tensions and even the apparent contradictions within *Sollicitudo*, as well as between *Sollicitudo* and other statements by this pope.

When we come across such tensions and apparent contradictions, we can logically attempt to explain them in several ways. If the contradictions are real and not merely apparent, one can say that the pope and those who assisted him in writing this and other documents are simply confused. Or one can say that the pope has changed his mind on some questions. The second suggestion is not necessarily either disrespectful or implausible. On the contrary, the whole idea of "refinement and development" in the Church's teaching assumes change, and such change must certainly include the mind of the Church's chief teacher. But in response to *Sollicitudo* some have asserted that the pope has changed his mind, in the sense of abandoning his previous positions, on, for example, Liberation Theology and Marxist ideology more generally. The plausibility of such a suggestion would seem to require some evidence internal or external to the text that the pope has in fact had a change of mind on these questions. There is no such evidence in *Sollicitudo* and, to the best of my knowledge, there is no external evidence of such a change.

Quite the opposite would seem to be the case. In order to illuminate the argument of *Sollicitudo*, John Paul cites his own earlier writings twenty-two times, and, as mentioned above, eight times invokes what CDF has said precisely on the issues most controverted in the interpretation of the present encyclical. And yet, on some questions, there is no denying the existence of tensions and apparent contradictions. In view of the pope's insistence that *Sollicitudo* be interpreted in the light of his teaching and the corpus of Roman Catholic social doctrine, these difficulties must, I conclude, be attributed to the fact that the present encyclical is not as precise as it could have been, and should have been. This means that we simply must work harder at understanding it. It also means that anyone who grabs a newspaper headline and passes it off as the gravamen of *Sollicitudo* is less interested in understanding than in exploiting this encyclical. Unfortunately, such partisan scoreboard readings of papal pronouncements are not uncommon.

Politics and Moral Agency

John Paul's stated intention, then, is to commemorate and develop *Populorum* within the context of Catholic social doctrine by offering "a fuller and more nuanced concept of development" (4). Adopting the language of the 1986 CDF Instruction on freedom and liberation, he wishes to offer " 'principles for reflection,' 'criteria of judgment' and 'directives for action' " (8). The distinction between "principles for reflection" and "criteria of judgment" is not always clear, while the "directives for action" are, in most instances, appropriately tentative and modest. The encyclical is intended not as a technical discussion or program of action but as a moral appeal. "In the context of these reflections, the decision to set out or to continue the journey involves, above all, a *moral* value which men and women of faith recognize as a demand of God's will, the only true foundation of an absolutely binding ethic" (38). It is God's will that we recognize great injustice and that, according to our several "vocations," we seek to redress that injustice. God has not revealed his will, and therefore the Church cannot speak authoritatively, with respect to which proposed remedies for injustice are to be adopted. We are called to examine our attitudes and behavior, indeed we are called to "conversion," and to trust "the power of his Spirit" in leading us to understand what such conversion might entail in practice (38). Certainly such conversion requires us to align ourselves with what the pope believes to be the great movement of our time: "Peoples and individuals aspire to be free" (46). Firmly, indeed adamantly, *Sollicitudo* states that freedom is "the first principle" in the right ordering of society. This accent on freedom is characteristic of John Paul and is grounded much more in his theological anthropology than in current political debates. Yet in those debates, on the basis of this letter, it should be obvious that the language about "peace and justice" must be changed to "freedom, peace, and justice." At the very least, it must be understood that justice without freedom is no justice at all.

Part V of the encyclical is titled "A Theological Reading of Modern Problems." In truth, this seems somewhat arbitrary since almost the entire document is pervaded by a theological reading. As a whole, *Sollicitudo* is an exercise in moral theology. The term "moral theology" is not defined in the text, but we know that in John Paul's thought it is very closely related to anthropology and the human aspiration toward freedom, which is finally the aspiration and destiny of communion with God. John Paul is the opponent of every form of determinism, and especially of anthropological determinisms, such as that proposed by Marxist doctrine. Human beings are moral agents, and

politics is viewed as a sphere of freedom for the exercise of that
moral agency. Thus the present encyclical declares that "the decisions which either accelerate or slow down the development
of peoples are really political in character." And to say that they
are political is to say that they are *"essentially moral decisions"*
(35). John Paul knows that questions such as development
"could seem extraneous to the legitimate concern of the
Church," but that view assumes a divorce between the moral
and the political that is not to be tolerated (8). Nor, in turn, can
the moral be divorced from that which is designated as religious
or theological. "For believers, and especially for Christians,
these [political and therefore moral] decisions will take their inspiration from the principles of faith, with the help of divine
grace" (35).

This is not to suggest that faith provides policy specifics. As
rational actors, Christians engage, like others, in "an objective
analysis of reality," but, unlike many others, from that analysis
they can derive what the pope describes as *"moral fact."* John
Paul suggests that the originality of *Populorum*, for instance, is
not in the way it reads the social and economic reality but in "the
moral evaluation" that it draws from that reading (9). The letter
may exaggerate the originality of *Populorum* in this respect, but
the basic line of thinking is clear enough: According to the anthropology of freedom, human beings are rational and moral
agents; rationally analyzing the social reality, they recognize the
moral fact of wrong; inspired by faith, they do not resign themselves to the wrong, but engaging in the sphere of moral agency
that is politics, and relying on divine assistance, they seek remedies for the wrong. And all this, as we shall see, is done under
the proviso of provisionality that marks a world far short of the
promised perfection in the coming Kingdom of God.

What then is the role of the Church, and of its teaching
authority, in support of this aspiration toward freedom? At first
the answer seems to be all-inclusive, even triumphalistic. After
alluding to the "realities" of the world, the economic and social
factors that hinder development, John Paul asserts, "In consequence, when the Church concerns herself with the 'development of peoples,' she cannot be accused of going outside her
own specific field of competence and, still less, outside the mandate received from the Lord" (8). One is led to ask whether there

is anything that is outside that competence and that mandate. In an important sense, the answer is no, but everything depends upon understanding how "the Church concerns herself." The Church does not concern herself by proposing solutions to every problem that comes down the turnpike. "The Church does not have *technical solutions* to offer for the problem of underdevelopment as such," the encyclical states. What the Church does do is to provoke and support "men and women [who] expend their efforts in search of the always relative happiness which is possible in this world, in line with their dignity as persons" (41).

Provoking and supporting involves, among other things, the effort to "awaken everyone's conscience" in order "to find a solution" to such perplexing problems as homelessness in the cities of the developed nations (17). *Sollicitudo* rightly alerts us to the fact that there is something terribly wrong, indeed scandalous, about, for instance, having thousands of homeless people on the streets of New York and our other major cities. Students of the subject agree that this problem is caused in largest part by factors such as the deinstitutionalizing of mental patients, a rampaging drug market, rigorous and perhaps unrealistic opposition to "interfering with the civil rights and individual preferences" of the homeless, and rent control and other state interventions that artificially constrict the housing market. Each of these is a "technical" problem and yet, at the same time, entails moral assumptions about the right ordering of society. The Church, according to John Paul, will not and should not prescribe how this problem of the homeless is to be resolved. Equally important, the Church will not and cannot let us resign ourselves to this situation or deny that it is a problem of moral urgency.

Far from being triumphalistic, the Church desires "to place herself at the service of the divine plan which is meant to order all things to the fullness which dwells in Christ (Col. 1:19) and which he communicated to his body." This expression underscores our reason for confidence in seeking policies appropriate to "the nature and characteristics of authentic human development" (31). We do not give up, because we believe there is indeed a "divine plan" of which our strivings are part. The Church, qua Church, responds "to her fundamental vocation of being a 'sacrament,' that is to say, 'a sign and instrument of intimate union with God and of the unity of the whole human race'" (31). There are those who might belittle such references to a divine plan and the Church's sacramental vocation as spiritual boilerplate, so to speak. But, as John Paul insists in this encyclical and elsewhere, without this "spiritual" self-understanding, everything the Church says and does is empty; it is no more than desperate do-goodism in the face of the doleful realities of the world. The word "vocation" is key. It is the Church's vocation to sustain many vocations. Vocation calls to vocation in a multifaceted world where each has his or her part, and yet all are part of a divine plan that has been revealed in advance in Jesus Christ and to which the Church bears witness.

In discussing the distinctive role and "competence" of the Church, it is perhaps noteworthy that the letter does not restate the "two powers" concept found in the encyclical he is commemorating. *Populorum* asserts: "Since the Church was founded to establish already here on earth the kingdom of heaven, but not to acquire earthly power, she openly affirms that there are two powers one distinct from the other, and that each of the two authorities, that is, the ecclesiastical and the civil, is supreme in its own sphere" (13). The two-powers concept is deeply rooted in Christian history, including the classic Reformation traditions, and its omission from *Sollicitudo* is intriguing. Of course the omission may be inadvertent, or perhaps it is because the concept is too closely tied to the "institutional model" of the Church (in Avery Dulles's term) that is no longer congruent with Roman Catholic ecclesiology. Or it may be that the two-powers concept is not helpful in clarifying the idea of the Church as the sacrament of universal solidarity that is at the heart of the present encyclical. Whatever the reason, the omission would seem to be not unimportant.

Persons and the Common Good

In *Sollicitudo*, the Church sacramentally testifies to that "solidarity" which is to mark—and is the final destiny of—the human community. "The exercise of solidarity within each society is valid when its members recognize one another as persons.

Those who are most influential, because they have a greater share of goods and common services, should feel responsible for the weaker and be ready to share with them all they possess." But solidarity also requires a mutuality in social duty. "Those who are weaker, for their part, in the same spirit of *solidarity*, should not adopt a purely *passive* attitude or one that is *destructive* of the social fabric, but, while claiming their legitimate rights, should do what they can for the good of all" (39). The distinctive role of the Church in the building of this solidarity is not to advance a "third way" between conflicting social systems. The Church's teaching, rather, "constitutes a *category of its own*" that stirs up promising possibilities in existing social orders and holds all such orders under a more ultimate judgment. The Church's aim is to "*interpret*" realities, "*to guide*" behavior, and always to point man towards his "vocation which is at once earthly and transcendent." The Church's teaching, therefore, "belongs to the field, not of *ideology*, but of *theology* and particularly of moral theology" (41).

As a moral agent, each person must reflect on his or her own responsibilities. The pope's role is essentially a modest one: "I wish to *appeal* with simplicity and humility to *everyone*, to all men and women without exception. I wish to ask them to be convinced of the seriousness of the present moment and of each one's individual responsibility, and to implement—by the way they live as individuals and as families, by the use of their resources, by their civic activity, by contributing to economic and political decisions and by personal commitment to national and international undertakings—the *measures* inspired by solidarity and love of preference for the poor" (47). This means, as *Sollicitudo* says at several points, giving what we have to the poor. That does not involve simply charity, in the pejorative sense in which that term is associated with the creation of dependency, but giving to the poor whatever knowledge and experience we may have that is useful in overcoming poverty. Such "giving," the letter makes clear, includes the encouragement of fair means of economic exchange.

Here again, vocations are very many and very different. Not everyone is a development expert, or charged with running refugee programs, or a statesman working on more just trade relations. Nor should everyone be directly involved in those tasks that appear to be most related to development. The encyclical appeals to us "to be convinced of the seriousness . . . of each one's individual responsibility," and we can be so convinced because we know that the fulfilling of our vocation—however directly or indirectly it may seem to be related to the tasks of development—is part of "the divine plan" alluded to earlier. If that transcendent truth is forgotten, the Church herself may appear to be "irrelevant." But that truth is remembered, and therefore we can say that in speaking as she does in this encyclical "The Church fulfills her mission to evangelize, for she offers her first contribution to the solution of the urgent problem of development when she proclaims the truth about Christ, about herself and about man, applying this truth to a concrete situation" (41). The "first contribution," then, is to "evangelize"—that is, to bring people into the orbit of faith in the "divine plan" revealed in Christ. This orbit is the space within the world for the reflection and judgment that equips us to act for the world.

Such action is not directed or controlled by Church authority. Again, the diversity of vocations is called to mind. "It is appropriate to emphasize the *preeminent role* that belongs to the *laity*, both men and women. . . . It is their task to animate temporal realities with Christian commitment, by which they show that they are witnesses and agents of peace and justice" (47). These words must be seen as an implicit censure of the older clericalized politics of "the Catholic state," and of the currently clericalized agitations for revolutionary change leading, in effect, to "a new Christendom." In addition, this animation of the temporal order depends also on non-Roman Catholic Christians, who, "through the Sacrament of Baptism and the profession of the same Creed, *share a real*, though imperfect, *communion* with us." The concern of the encyclical, says John Paul, will be familiar to all Christians, "for these motives are inspired by the Gospel of Jesus Christ." Likewise, he invites the cooperation of Jews and Muslims and all people of religious faith, for the concern set forth in the document "depends on our *fidelity* to our vocation as men and women of faith." And it depends on men and women of faith because "it depends, above all, *on God*" (47). If this theme is not allowed to occupy center stage—this theme of transcendence, of human aspiration toward the freedom that is perfect communion with God—any interpretation of *Sollicitudo* will be a grave misinterpretation. Such misinterpretations may cleverly paste together rhetorical snatches in support of diverse programs of change, but they will have missed the animating inspiration of John Paul's message in this encyclical and elsewhere.

The theological and anthropological postulate of the human aspiration toward freedom necessarily highlights the role of "creativity" in development. In "every form of totalitarianism" and in every society that pursues a false notion of equality that is contrary to the common good, we witness the diminution or destruction of "the spirit of initiative, that is to say *the creative subjectivity of the citizen*" (15). This understanding of creativity and its relationship to freedom is a critical "criterion of judgment" with respect to justice within and between societies. John Paul emphatically and repeatedly rejects the notion—once very common and still advanced by some—that a choice must be made between bread and freedom. While freedom does not guarantee development, the absence of freedom does guarantee the absence of development. In one's concern for the poor, says the letter, "one must not overlook that *special form of poverty* which consists in being deprived of fundamental human rights, in particular the right to religious freedom and also the right to freedom of economic initiative" (42). Even if material development were possible at the price of sacrificing the freedom and respect due the human person, the encyclical goes so far as to say, such an achievement "will prove unsatisfying and in the end contemptible" (33).

Sollicitudo becomes very specific with respect to the requirements of freedom as they touch upon "the criteria of judgment" for the just ordering of society. The much-derided "bourgeois" civil, political, and human rights are seen as inescapable imperatives in the light of man's "transcendent vocation." At one point the encyclical provides a short catalog of what is required: "the right to life at every stage of its existence; the rights of the family as the basic social community, or 'cell of society'; justice in employment relationships; the rights inherent in the life of the political community as such; the rights based on the *transcendent vocation* of the human being, beginning with the right of freedom to profess and practice one's own religious belief" (33). With similar specificity, the pope notes the importance of private human rights groups, rigorously independent of government control, for the monitoring of human rights (26). Here the pope would clearly seem to be offering the Church's support for private human rights efforts that have been crushed or harassed in places as various as the Soviet Union, Eastern Europe, Nicaragua, and Chile.

Development and Solidarity

As mentioned earlier, the distinction between "principles for reflection" and "criteria of judgment" is not spelled out. But, whether it be a principle or criterion, the concept of distributive justice finds expression at a number of points in *Sollicitudo* . We witness an *"unequal distribution"* of the world's goods (9); there is a "widening gap" between rich and poor, both between and within nations (14); justice requires a "fair distribution of the results of true development" (26); one of the greatest injustices is that "the ones who possess much are relatively *few* and those who possess almost nothing are *many*" (28); and so forth. While cognate language is employed, distributive justice is not articulated as a principle. Certainly no formula is proposed for what might constitute a just distribution of goods. And, as we have seen, John Paul specifically cautions against a "false equality" that violates the "creativity" that is appropriate to human freedom and the necessary condition of "authentic development." The possession of goods is not evil; in fact, one critical dimension of development is aimed at the poor coming into such possession. "The evil does not consist in 'having' as such, but in possessing without regard for the *quality* and the *ordered hierarchy* of the goods one has" (28). A zero-sum approach to material well-being, in which it is assumed that the possessions of one are necessarily at the expense of the poverty of another, can find no support in *Sollicitudo*. Equally, there is no support for—indeed there is a clear condemnation of—the idea that material well-being is not accompanied by an obligation to those not-so-well off.

The intuition of distributive justice seems to find its clearest expression in the demands for freedom and participation. The freedom to participate must be amply distributed both within and between nations. For instance, the encyclical asserts that "either *all* the nations of the world participate, or it will not be true development" (17). Of course the pope knows that it is not an all-or-nothing proposition in the sense that no nation can materially develop without the participation of all. His point, rather, is that the development of some, if they are indifferent to the other, is not "true development." And it is not true development because it violates that "solidarity" of humanity which is a recurring concern of *Sollicitudo*. Distributive justice in this encyclical, then, must be understood in terms of freedom, participation, and responsibility. The last note, that of responsibility, is struck most clearly in the document's treatment of the parable of the talents (30).

Referring back to his encyclical *Laborem Exercens*, John Paul underscores work as the responsibility of cocreativity with God the Creator. "It is always man who is the protagonist of development," he asserts. The servant who hides the gift he has received, no matter how small that gift, comes under divine judgment as a "wicked and slothful servant." If we do not "sow" and "reap," if we do not create with what we have been given, "even what we have will be taken away from us," says John Paul. Translated into the terms of a long-standing debate in this country, the idea of distributive justice in *Sollicitudo* would seem to be squarely on the side of "equality of opportunity" rather than "equality of result." At the same time, however, John Paul would emphasize that genuine equality in the opportunity to participate requires constant attention on the part of all to the institutions of freedom. The participation that is required by this concept of distributive justice does not happen naturally and is only imperfectly realized everywhere. In addition, those who, for whatever reason, do not avail themselves of such opportunity cannot be read out of the community for which we are morally responsible without grievously violating the "solidarity" of our common humanity.

Distributive justice as participation is extended also to relations between nations. The idea of the nation is somewhat ambiguous in this document. *Populorum* flatly condemned "nationalism," along with racism and other evils. His experience as a son of Poland likely has some bearing on John Paul's appreciation of positive aspects in national identity and allegiance. Although the text wraps the phrase in quotation marks, it speaks of the "rights of individual nations" (15). "In fact, it often happens that a nation is deprived of its subjectivity, that is to say the 'sovereignty' which is its right," the document asserts. It goes on to underscore the pluralistic character of a nation, including economic, political, social, and cultural dimensions. In this connection John Paul condemns the seizure of power by any one group, "as happens in every form of totalitarianism."

In a pluralistic world, the "rights of individual nations" seem to be highly differentiated between rich and poor nations. Put somewhat too simply, the poor nations have claims to make and the rich nations have obligations to fulfill. To be sure, *Sollicitudo* cautions poor nations against the dangers of dependency in living on the dole. "Each of them must act in accordance with its own responsibilities, *not expecting everything* from the more favored countries," it is said (44). The temptation of rich nations, on the other hand, is to isolationism. "If a nation were to succumb more or less deliberately to the temptation to close in upon itself and failed to meet the responsibilities following from its superior position in the community of nations, it *would fall seriously short* of its clear ethical duty" (23). While the "favored" nations are exhorted to what might be termed constructive intervention, they are repeatedly cautioned that they must serve, and never violate, the cultural and political integrity of the poorer nations.

Absent from *Sollicitudo* is any developed notion of national interest. More precisely, it is implied that "national interest" has moral status only in the case of nations in need. But one must ask whether the most developed countries do not also have legitimate needs—indeed, needs which they are morally bound not to neglect. It is not necessary to belong to the "realist" school of international relations—represented by, for example, Reinhold Niebuhr and Hans Morgenthau—to be puzzled by the suggestion of *Sollicitudo* that nations, like individuals, should base their policies upon altruism. In international organizations (presumably the United Nations is intended) the encyclical urges "the overcoming of political rivalries and the renouncing of all desire to manipulate these organizations, which exist solely for *the common good*" (43). True, the present document, unlike *Populorum*, gives no encouragement to the idea of world government replacing nation states, and is in fact sharply critical of aspects of *"international organizations."* Like *Populorum*, however, it fails to recognize that the purpose of international relations is not to overcome political rivalries but to *order* political rivalries in a way that makes peace and mutual progress more secure.

A clear idea of the moral status of the nation and of "national interest rightly understood" is sorely missing here and in other papal documents. One result is to weaken the plausibility of papal exhortations to the nations. Those responsible for the administration of "politics among nations" (Morgenthau) are not likely to say so publicly, but they are too frequently confirmed in their sometimes cynical suspicion that the Church is simply "moralizing" rather than offering moral guidance. The problem should not be exaggerated. There is much in *Sollicitudo* that is applicable to the conduct of international relations. But the lack of a clearer understanding of "nation" and of "national interest" is a deficiency that one hopes will be remedied in the further development of the Church's social teaching. It is a subject that cannot be omitted from a moral theology that intends to provide principles for reflection, criteria of judgment, and directives for action. The phrase "moral man and immoral society" (Niebuhr) puts it too starkly, but it is nonetheless true that societies are not moral agents in the same way that persons are. It is homiletically effective but practically misleading to suggest, for instance, that the relationship between rich and poor nations is analogous to that between Dives and Lazarus. Oddly enough, the distinction between the moral agency of social structures and the moral agency of persons is one that this pope has emphasized elsewhere, and emphasizes again in this encyclical's discussion of "sin" and "structure." It is a distinction that one hopes will be developed further with respect to nations and national interest.

Closely related to that question is some conceptual untidiness in the encyclical's insistent emphasis upon the *"interdependence"* of nations of the world. On the one hand, the pope accepts what many believe to be the distorting imagery of the First, Second, Third, and Fourth Worlds. Those alleged divisions, we are told, are signs of "fragmentation." The alternative is *"interdependence,"* but that too has *"disastrous consequences"* if separated from "its ethical requirements" (17). Enter the hegemony of the "two blocs," which presumably effects greater interdependence, but in a manner "separated from its ethical requirements" (17). The problem is that the blocs impose themselves ("Each of the two blocs harbors in its own way a tendency towards *imperialism*") in a way that violates "autonomous nations" (22). Here, it seems, we find ourselves in a tangle. To be freed from it we need, once again, a clearer understanding of the nation and of politics among nations. It is not easy to understand how or why there should be "autonomous" nations in an "interdependent" world, or why associations between nations, entered upon for reasons of mutual benefit, should require the pejorative "imperialism" (however qualified) when the association involves a "great power."

Distributive justice as participation requires such association among nations. *Sollicitudo* would be more helpful if it clarified, at least in principle, which kinds of association are, and which are not, "separated from [their] ethical requirements" (17). The letter explicitly rejects the false egalitarianism that would put all relations within society on an equal footing, and that presumably extends to relations between nations. It would be useful to indicate where the line is crossed and *"autonomous nations"* end up as "parts of a machine, cogs on a gigantic wheel" (22). Once again, critically important distinctions are missing. Of course the absent distinction that is most remarked is that between the nature and purpose of the "two blocs." Others in this symposium will no doubt comment on that. With respect to this encyclical I would only draw attention to the assertion toward the end that "the Church does not propose economic and political systems or programs, nor does she show preference for one or the other, provided that human dignity is properly respected and promoted, and provided she herself is allowed the room she needs to exercise her ministry in the world" (41).

Provided that. The coherence of the statement turns on those two words. The same two words make it clear that *Sollicitudo* is not proposing a "moral equivalence" between free and unfree social orders. Any fair reading must acknowledge, I believe, that "provided that" cancels out the words "nor does she show preference." But then one must ask why the encyclical employs such a convoluted construction that requires such effort to read it fairly. "Between the Cosa Nostra and the Red Cross I have no preference, provided that both are law abiding and serve the common good." That statement makes little contribution, and the first part, removed from its context, can only sow confusion. Unless one is prepared to believe that John Paul has dramatically changed his mind or is simply befuddled (neither of which we have reason to believe), the context of his own writing must be permitted to guide our interpretation of such controverted passages.

As we have seen, within this very encyclical there is set forth at several points the "criteria of judgment" with respect to what constitutes societal justice. In addition, the letter repeatedly cites the 1984 and 1986 instructions of CDF on liberation and freedom which (especially the 1986 instruction) are much more detailed on the subject of democratic values. In his earlier encyclical, "On Human Work," the pope declared that the Church's teaching on justice "diverges radically from the program of collectivism as proclaimed by Marxism." (He also says it "differs" from the "rigid capitalism" practiced by early liberalism, a capitalism which, as the pope surely knows, bears little similarity to the economic systems of the United States, Sweden, France, or of the Italy that surrounds the Vatican.) The encyclical "The Holy Spirit in the Church and the World" is, if it is possible, even more explicit. It declares that resistance to the Holy Spirit "reaches its clearest expression in materialism, both in its theoretical form as a system of thought, and in its practical form as a method of interpreting and evaluating facts, and likewise as a program of corresponding conduct. The system which has developed most and carried to extreme practical consequences this form of thought, ideology, and praxis is dialectical and historical materialism, which is still recognized as the essential core of Marxism." That system of materialism is "essentially and systematically atheistic [and] radically excludes the presence and action of God, who is spirit, in the world and above all in man."

These are hardly the words of one who shows no preference between a system based on the principles of Marxist-Leninism and one based on constitutional democracy and human rights. The imperfections of Western democracies are evident to all, and the pope is right to draw our attention to them once again. It is as unfortunate as it is inexplicable that in doing so he uses language that allows itself to be exploited, as it is being widely exploited, to obscure his own teaching. That teaching has to do with matters even more important than East-West rivalries, the contest between totalitarianism and democracy, or theories of development. It has to do with the anthropological and philosophical foundations of John Paul's entire moral theology. While it is understandable, indeed imperative, that the Church distance itself from the partisan conflicts of the great powers, it is ironic that, in trying to do precisely that, *Sollicitudo* at several points plays into the hand of those who champion causes against which this pope has declared himself in no uncertain terms.

What the pope is against is always determined by the "principles of reflection and criteria of judgment" controlling what he is for. What he is for is the freedom that is appropriate "to man's divine likeness and to his vocation to immortality." This the encyclical calls "the *transcendent reality* of the human being" that issues from the creation of a man and a woman, thereby indicating that the human reality is "fundamentally social" (29). The theme of creation is, as noted earlier, closely linked to the importance the letter places upon "creativity," also in economic development. Human creativity is to be seen "as a moment in the story which began at creation"; it is the continuing creation. But it is not an uninterrupted story, for it is constantly endangered by "infidelity to the Creator's will, and especially by the temptation to idolatry." Defeatism before the difficulties encountered in development is also a form of idolatry, the substituting of our judgment for God's. Those who renounce or resign the task are "betraying the will of God the Creator" (30).

An optimism based upon a purely secular idea of progress, however, can also be such a betrayal. Genuine progress and hope are only possible because of God's promise given us in Christ (31). It is God's love for us that makes it possible to base development "on the love of God and neighbor" that can become, in a favored expression of Paul VI, the "civilization of love" (33). There are at a number of points in *Sollicitudo* rhetorical crescendos in which everything—development, love, peace, liberation, justice—is summed up in the word "solidarity." These expressions do not always repay analytical examination, since they are apparently employed chiefly for effect. To say, for example, that solidarity is the way to peace does not add much of substance once peace has been defined as a part of solidarity. John Paul is much given to expressing himself pleonastically, and it is frequently very effective indeed. In the present case almost everything positive is another word for "solidarity." The insistent use of that term, with its most particular meaning in the recent history of Poland, is yet another signal that it is important to understand *Sollicitudo* as it would be read within that system of unfreedom.

Structures and Sin

There is much comment, and much protest, in connection with what the encyclical says about "structures of sin." Some of the protest has been, I believe, excessive It should be readily acknowledged that every human structure is marked by the sinfulness of fallen humanity. And yet it is troubling when the encyclical speaks of "superdevelopment" and the "miseries of underdevelopment" as being "equally inadmissible." This is the occasion of the document's strictures against the "blind submission to pure consumerism" (28). It seems that the pope intends to warn against the classic vice of gluttony, and that warning is of course always in order. But his warning descends into a description of life in the "superdeveloped" countries that few Americans, for example, would recognize as an accurate version of how they actually live. "An object already owned but now superseded by something better is discarded," we are told, "with no thought of its possible lasting value in itself, nor of some other human being who is poorer."

It is hard to know what to make of that. Does *Sollicitudo* refer to automobiles, television sets, computers, clothing, or what? Surely a television set has little, if any, "lasting value in itself." One wonders if the author of this section is aware of the practice of trading things in, or of the Salvation Army, Volunteers of America, and hundreds of thousands of second-hand stores. And surely there is some necessary connection between replacing things and production, which in turn is closely related to employment and all the other issues addressed by this encyclical under the rubric of "development." (If this and similar passages were actually written by the pope, one cannot help but wonder from whom he has received his impression of life in the "superdeveloped" countries. One hopes it is not from television, where, if one were to believe the commercials, people are forever hopping out of their easy chairs and rushing off in a frenzy to buy the latest widget.)

On the other hand, maybe the encyclical is not referring to American life at all. One of the frustrations with *Sollicitudo* is its level of generalizations when presumably offering a concrete reading of current "realities of the world." It is hard to believe, however, that the references to "superdevelopment" do not point also, if not mainly, to the United States. In any event, the superficial and inaccurate descriptions offered distract attention from the moral theology of the pope's message. Certainly a contemporary form of gluttony may be described as "consumerism." But with respect to the moral dangers of material prosperity, *Populorum* included an important note that is missing from the present encyclical. Quoting *Gaudium et Spes*, Paul VI asserted: "it is not thereby said that this temporal prosperity in itself hampers the activity of the soul, nay rather blessed with it 'man's spirit, increasingly freed from the bondage of the material, can more readily be drawn to the worship and contemplation of the Creator'" (14).

Sollicitudo would likewise direct man to communion with the Creator, and elsewhere underscores that this is not in conflict with "Man the protagonist" but precisely requires human engagement in what may be termed the continuing creative work of God. The problem is sin, and sin, said Martin Luther (who is not quoted by the pope), is the creation turned in upon itself and away from the Creator. *Sollicitudo* makes clear that sin is evident in the behavior of all people, but, for some unexplained reason, reserves the discussion of "structures of sin" for the problem of a world "divided into blocs" (36). The pope underscores, as he has before, that structures of sin "are rooted in personal sin." In this sense it would seem that all human institutions are, at least in part, structures of sin. One looks for, but does not find, any reference to the Church, insofar as it is a human institution, as a structure of sin. With reference to the Church—and at some points to religion more generally—there seems to be an exemption from the pervasive moral ambiguity that attends all human activity and institutions. That the Church is an ambiguous "sacrament" of the solidarity for which the encyclical calls may be inferred from its exhortation that Christians and also church leadership need to be radically changed, even converted.

There are other difficulties in the discussion of structural sin. In a longish footnote, John Paul reiterates that social and structural sin is "the result of the accumulation and concentration of many *personal sins.*" It is not evident how this is conceptually related to moral demands and censures placed upon institutions such as nations, as we discussed earlier. John Paul is a personalist and therefore, as already noted, an enemy of determinisms that would eliminate personal moral agency. In his own encyclicals and apostolic exhortations, as well as in the CDF documents he invokes, there is strong and justified suspicion of terms such as "systemic evil," "structural sin," "social guilt," and so forth. Such expressions, which are found chiefly in the language of the ideological Left, obscure the "person-sized" scale of moral warfare. They also provide, as the pope says, "specious reasons" by which individual people excuse themselves from moral responsibility for the wrongs of the world. "The real responsibility, then, lies with individuals," he writes. "A situation—or likewise an institution, a structure, society itself—is not itself the subject of moral acts. Hence a situation cannot in itself be good or bad" (36, n. 65). (Of course "good" and "bad" here refer to moral categories.)

In this connection too one looks for further development and clarification in papal teaching. Within this encyclical it would seem that situations and institutions are addressed in terms of moral agency. And while the emphasis on personal moral agency and responsibility is to be welcomed, the way in which it is expressed here is only with difficulty made consonant with papal statements elsewhere—with, for example, the critique of Marxist systems mentioned earlier. John Paul would certainly seem to believe that certain anthropological propositions—whether of freedom or unfreedom—can be embodied in an institution or system, which then becomes in a limited sense "the subject of moral acts" that can constrict "the real responsibility" that "lies with individuals" (36). Even the present encyclical speaks of "the 'structures of sin' and the sins which they produce" (39). So it would seem that institutions can be "subjects of moral acts" after all. What would seem to be required is a more thorough analysis of the symbiotic relationship between personal sin and the institutional consequences of such sin as it affects both the original subject of the sinful decision and those who are made objects of its consequences. In any event, some readers of this encyclical may be puzzled as to why it adopts a phrase such as "structures of sin," only to add in a long footnote that it does not mean what those who coined and gave currency to the phrase claim it means—and what most people will undoubtedly take it to mean.

Awaiting the Kingdom

Finally, one must ask whether *Sollicitudo* can be justly criticized for being utopian. Utopianism is endemic to moral discourse on political, economic, and social questions. Utopianism is marked by an effort to wish the world away, or to wish another world into existence. It frequently ends up with the truism of asserting that the world would be a much nicer place if the world were a much nicer place. It is typically an exercise in moralizing rather than moral analysis. It nurtures impossible expectations that result in dangerous frustrations. *Populorum Progressio* was widely criticized for being utopian. Even *Sollicitudo* suggests that it was excessively "optimistic." Of course there are many who are prepared to dismiss as utopian any religious statement about the right ordering of "the real world."

There are passages in the present encyclical that might warrant the suspicion of utopianism. Quoting *Populorum*, it is asserted that "in a different world, ruled by concern for the *common good* of all humanity, or by concern for the 'spiritual and human development of all' instead of by the quest for individual profit, peace would be *possible* as the result of a 'more perfect justice among people'" (10). In a different world, indeed. And we have already discussed passages that seem to suggest that nations should transcend the imperatives of national interest. At several points it is indicated that poorer nations should interact in an interdependent world with richer nations, but without having their cultural integrity affected by that interaction. How this can be, contrary to the entire history of interaction between peoples, is not explained. In addition, there is at times a note of romanticism about the history and culture of poor nations, which would seem to disregard the fact that those histories and cultures are sometimes antithetical to the moral goods that *Sollicitudo* says should mark a just society and a just world. The pope surely is not urging, for example, respect for the practice of suttee, or for the religious intolerance of Islamic cultures, or for the racial, tribal, and ethnic discriminations which are foundational to the identities of many, perhaps most, peoples in the world. Surely not, and yet "the criteria of judgment" relevant to what should be respected and preserved and what should not are unhappily missing.

But there is also much in *Sollicitudo* that counters the charge of utopianism, romanticism, and wishful thinking. There is a sharp criticism of the delusion of automatic and limitless progress in human history. "Such an idea . . . now seems to be seriously called into doubt, particularly since the tragic experience of the two world wars, the planned and partly achieved destruction of whole peoples, and the looming atomic peril. A naive *mechanistic optimism* has been replaced by a well-founded anxiety for the fate of humanity" (27). John Paul would replace such naive optimism with a specifically Christian faith and confidence. Although the Church knows the evil of which man is capable, she also has confidence in man, he writes. This is because man still bears the image of the Creator, and our creativity participates in his. Also, no matter how grim the outlook, God works in mysterious ways, as it is said. In a footnote we encounter again the "O felix culpa" which has become a hallmark of John Paul's writing—the "happy fault" by which God turns evil into good.

As for confidence in the possibility of overcoming present injustices, the encyclical affirms: "Ultimately, this confidence and this possibility are based on the *Church's awareness* of the divine promise guaranteeing that our present history does not remain closed in upon itself but is open to the Kingdom of God" (47). Or again: "The Church well knows that *no temporal achievement* is to be identified with the Kingdom of God, but that all such achievements simply *reflect* and in a sense *anticipate* the glory of the Kingdom, the Kingdom which we await at the end of history, when the Lord will come again" (48). It is this eschatological horizon that distinguishes the entire document from utopianism and its attendant errors. This ultimate hope finds expression in the prayer that brings the encyclical to its conclusion: "By sharing the good things you give us, may we secure justice and equality for every human being, an end to all division and a human society built on love and peace." Only those who think faith is utopian and prayer is wishful thinking will deny the "realism" of this declaration of challenge and hope.

I have not concealed disappointment with aspects of *Sollicitudo*. The criteria of judgment, so to speak, on which disappointment is based are the earlier writings, including the earlier encyclicals, of John Paul, plus the enormous and continuing promise of his moral and spiritual leadership among Christians and in the entire world. *Sollicitudo* is at many points conceptually ragged and argumentatively disjointed. It thus lends itself to being used to diametrically opposite purposes, and to purposes which I am confident are opposite to its intent. The conflicting headlines mentioned at the beginning of this essay can both find warrant in the text of this encyclical. As can yet others. One hopes that the resulting confusion will lead people to read the encyclical itself to find out just what it does say. Unfortunately, it is not easy reading, and even those who have the patience to study it carefully will discover that not all the obscurities are dissipated.

I have tried to offer a faithful, although admittedly incomplete, reading of the moral and theological argument advanced. Others have, and no doubt more will, come up with different readings. One can only hope that all who attempt to interpret *Sollicitudo* will follow the hermeneutical rule of letting the text interpret itself as much as possible—and will let the ambiguities of this text be interpreted by the structure of the argument more effectively set forth by John Paul on other occasions.

The Writing of an Encyclical

ROBERTO SURO

Pope John Paul II has long remained aloof from the Vatican bureaucracy, but when he set out to redefine the Roman Catholic view of global politics with his recent encyclical, *Sollicitudo Rei Socialis*, he made an unusual effort to give Vatican policymakers a voice in developing the document, according to senior church officials.

"Lots of people wanted to see their particular concerns addressed in the encyclical, and the Pope tried to accommodate a good number of them at the expense of clarity and logic," said one official. "So many were given a chance to influence the text that it became a real institutional document, but the presence of so many hands also ensured that one hand, the Pope's, was clearly dominant in the end."

John Paul laid out the basic themes of the encyclical at the start of a drafting process that began last June. Lengthy consultations followed within the Vatican and with outside experts as successive drafts were prepared. But, Vatican officials said, many changes were made, and a variety of specific arguments only took final shape during several weeks of hurried labor in January after the document was already overdue.

Some major questions were decided at virtually the last minute. Officials said that a debate persisted over whether to include a standard distinction in Catholic social doctrine between capitalist systems which are capable of self-correction and Marxist systems which are not. The self-correction concept was left out in an effort to be evenhanded with both sides.

159

The complex and sometimes clumsy process used to write the document, including its rushed finale, is blamed by some within the Vatican for a text that is not as good as it might have been and that has left the document open to criticisms that distract from its central message. Even so, the method used to write this encyclical did accomplish one of John Paul's central goals for the document.

Most of the pope's recent predecessors had at one time or another been creatures of the Roman Curia, the Vatican bureaucracy of secretariats, commissions, congregations, and councils that is the central administrative body of the Church. John Paul took over this institution as an outsider, and he has largely remained one, primarily defining his pontificate with initiatives that do not greatly involve the Curia, especially his trips abroad.

This encyclical more than any of the six that preceded it is a product of collaboration between the pope and the Curia. *Sollicitudo Rei Socialis* is most definitely John Paul's document, but when he set out to make radical propositions he made a conscious effort to seriously involve the Vatican's top leaders and ensure that the document was also theirs.

Issued to the public on 19 February, the encyclical defines a new "international outlook" for Catholic social doctrine that is rooted in the concerns of the Third World. Church officials said the pope wanted to be sure that the Vatican's top prelates shared this outlook from the start.

A pope exercises his supreme teaching authority in writing an encyclical, and these documents have always been officially described as solely the work of popes, even though inside the small, gossipy world of the Vatican the hunt for alleged ghostwriters starts well before an encyclical comes out.

Talking to an outsider, especially one who intends to publish his findings, Vatican officials exercise maximum reserve when the subject is the writing of an encyclical. I found that the game of cat and mouse, of hint and obfuscation, was even more intense than on subjects that might seem more sensitive. Discussing who, other than the pope, was involved in casting the document is the sort of topic that causes senior officials to stop in mid-sentence when an assistant comes into the room.

Still, three persons who actually handled the text and helped put words on paper at different stages of the process did agree to tell me something about how this encyclical came into being. None of them was totally forthcoming and all of them insisted on remaining rigidly anonymous, as did several other Vatican officials who were more peripherally involved.

Mysteries are bound to persist in a situation like this, and even officials who took part in the drafting wonder whether the pope had other helpers whose names remain unknown. In future years, church historians will develop a fuller and perhaps more accurate account of these events. That has happened with other encyclicals before but sometimes not until after the papal author has died. For the moment, then, this is what we know.

The best starting point for the story of *Sollicitudo Rei Socialis* seems to be 3 April 1987. John Paul was in Chile. On a crisp, sunny afternoon of Southern Hemisphere autumn a solemn Mass was held in a Santiago park to crown the pope's trip. But the event took a tragic turn even as nearly one million worshipers were gathering. Anti-government protestors clashed with police during a hit-and-run riot which lasted throughout the service and left nearly thirty persons badly injured. The air in Parque O'Higgins smelled of tear gas, not incense, and guns instead of bells sounded in the distance.

When the long liturgy ended at nightfall, John Paul seemed unwilling to leave. He repeatedly paused to stare at the violence unfolding before him even as aides tried to usher him off the altar towards a heavily guarded motorcade.

What went through his mind at that moment only he can say, but some officials who are close to him believe the riot in Parque O'Higgins, by far the worst violence during any of his public appearances, provided an impetus for the writing of the encyclical.

Joaquin Navarro Valis, the pope's spokesman, noted in another context that "this man thinks in terms of ideas, not images, even when very vivid things are happening around him." One could argue that all the ideas at the core of the encyclical were acted out very dramatically that afternoon.

Using the simplest of geopolitical terms, the encyclical portrays the world as dominated by a dialectical clash between East and West which threatens peace and retards the South's economic and moral development. This clash was played out by the youths waving the banners of left-wing revolutionary groups and the "Carabineros" that keep order for General

Augusto Pinochet, Chile's right-wing dictator. The encyclical's response to this division is encapsulated in the brief words John Paul improvised that afternoon: "Love is stronger."

In chatting with aides afterwards the pope seemed most impressed by the hundreds of thousands of faithful who kept praying at their own peril, and the pope often had those people in mind as he wrote the encyclical, according to one official. "He had thought about doing this encyclical before," said one official, "and one reason he decided to revive the project was because he felt that Catholics like those who kept with him in the Parque O'Higgins deserved clear direction from the church on how to find a way out of the turmoil and poverty around them."

General Pinochet's fourteen-year dictatorship has accentuated a split among Catholics in Chile that is evident across Latin America. The division is most clearly evident in attitudes towards liberation theology, a school of thought that calls on the church radically to transform itself so that it can become an aggressive agent of social change.

Liberation theology has also been a very controversial topic within the Vatican. Top officials have debated what is the best response to a movement seen as a grave challenge to the church on the most Catholic of continents. In 1984 and 1986, the Vatican issued major documents on liberation theology that condemned its frequent reliance on Marxist analysis and its attacks on existing church structures.

John Paul, perhaps more than any other pope, has spoken out for the poor and the powerless, but proponents of liberation theology have sometimes cast him as a defender of the established order. As a kind of indirect response, the pope promised on several occasions to present eventually the positive side of this theology, and he finally did with this encyclical.

Last summer, when the document was taking shape, John Paul read books on liberation theology and reread others, according to an official who was invited to discuss the subject with the pope. The encyclical itself rewrites the slogan "a preferential option for the poor" as a *love of preference* for the poor" (42). And, as Peter Hebblethwaite of the *National Catholic Reporter* has noted, it makes use of several biblical passages that are frequently cited by liberation theology authors.

"This encyclical offers a new liberation theology," said Rocco

Buttiglione, an Italian political philosopher who is close to the pope. "It is a new Liberation Theology that surpasses the limits of the old one that is so thoroughly grounded in the Latin American experience and it is a theology that knows Communists."

In the past the pope has severely criticized liberation theology for focusing on a concept of material liberation instead of the spiritual salvation that is the church's real goal. This encyclical does not compromise that stand, but instead seems to offer a new synthesis of salvation and earthly liberation.

This is a form of liberation that applies not just to those trapped by the constraints of the Third World. Thus, the encyclical drew another impetus from the pope's trip to Poland last June, according to several officials. There he saw a people in need of a liberation theology as much as the Chileans. In his speech at the Catholic University of Lublin, the pope added a new chapter to his analysis of man's subjectivity as an aspect of the human identity defined in Genesis which established his freedom of choice. This address, and his talks to workers on the Baltic Coast on solidarity as a concept of Catholic social doctrine, seem to prefigure essential aspects of the encyclical.

It was after his return from Poland on 14 June that the pope set in motion the machinery that eventually produced *Sollicitudo Rei Socialis*, and much of the drafting took place after the pope's September visit to the United States, another nation that he feels is in need of liberation because it is being corrupted by an abundance he calls *"superdevelopment"* (28).

The result is a document that is both theological and political, both abstract and practical, as it tries to present a model for development that applies as much to those who have too much as to those who have too little. "The danger with a document like this that tries so hard to be addressed to all nations," said one Vatican official, "is that it ends up being addressed to no one."

Back in the Vatican in early summer, John Paul began working out the major points he wanted to make in the encyclical. Writing early in the morning before receiving officials and visitors or in the evenings after dinner, he produced what in the Vatican was called "la schema." More than a simple outline but much less than a first draft, it laid out the basic ideas of the document in chunks of prose.

Despite the many changes to follow, the final version

develops in detail most of the basic concepts already articulated
at this early stage. Other ideas like the pope's analysis of the relationship between population growth and development were
reduced to brief passages.

The standard process for producing encyclicals usually requires that the text be checked by the Congregation for the Doctrine of the Faith, the Vatican's guardian of orthodoxy, led by
Joseph Cardinal Ratzinger. Assistance in drafting and the final
editing normally comes from the powerful Secretariat of State,
the Vatican's general staff, headed by Agostino Cardinal
Casaroli. In addition, John Paul, like other popes, has called in
theologians and scholars when expertise was needed in specific
fields, such as the historians who helped him with *Slavorum
Apostoli*, the 1985 encyclical on Saints Cyril and Methodius, who
converted the Slavs.

All of John Paul's previous encyclicals have primarily con-
veyed his theological reflections on a given subject, but *Sollicitudo Rei Socialis* is more like a broad policy document giving the
church directives on a variety of big issues. Right from the start
John Paul adopted a procedure for the writing of this encyclical
that reflected its scope and his apparent intent that it enjoy the
broadest possible support within the Vatican.

Coordination of the project and responsibility for early drafting were entrusted to the Pontifical Commission for Justice and
Peace, the Vatican body that concentrates on questions of social
doctrine. The pope's "schema," or a text that was developed
from it, was distributed by the Secretariat of State to the chiefs
of several other important Vatican offices, who were asked to
offer comments and revisions.

Those queried surely included Cardinals Ratzinger and
Casaroli as well as Archbishop Achille Silvestrini, chief of the
Council for the Public Affairs of the Church, the Vatican's foreign ministry, and Cardinal Jozef Tomko, prefect of the Congregation for the Propagation of the Faith, which oversees mission-
ary activities. The responses were collated at Justice and Peace,
where the first draft of the document was put together and then
sent to the pope.

This process of sending out versions of the text for comments
and then attempting to work in the suggestions was repeated
several times as the document moved towards completion. As

a result, the two prelates who run Justice and Peace, both men who have known the pope for twenty-five years or more, played key roles in shaping the encyclical in the early stages. The commission's president is Roger Cardinal Etchegaray, a longtime archbishop of Marseilles who was a close friend of that city's late mayor and political boss, Gaston Defferre, a Socialist. Archbishop Jorge Maria Mejia of Argentina is the commission's secretary.

Both these officials had overseen preparation of the commission's December 1986 document on international debt, which weighed the responsibilities of developing and creditor nations. According to several officials, that project started focusing the pope's attention on the need to update Catholic social doctrine in terms of new global issues. These two officials were also responsible for the formal celebration in March 1987 of the twentieth anniversary of Pope Paul VI's encyclical *Populorum Progressio*, which John Paul commemorates in this document. In addition, Justice and Peace conducted a survey of bishops' conferences on development issues in the light of the two decades that had passed since *Populorum Progressio*, and the results were passed on to the pope for use in preparing the encyclical.

While the early text of *Sollicitudo Rei Socialis* was circulating, John Paul repeatedly sought out the Curia's ideas first-hand to discuss aspects of the documents. On other occasions, the pope would raise an issue without ever letting his visitors know he was writing an encyclical. Regardless, his intellectual approach was the same. "He does this often," said the official, "asking questions that provoke you to carry out your train of thought. He listens and then perhaps at the end he offers his own synthesis."

Not all seminars took place within the Curia. John Paul had many meals and informal audiences with prelates who visited Rome for the Synod of Bishops last fall, and he often asked them about issues raised by the writing of the encyclical. The director general of the International Monetary Fund, Michael Camdessus, spent almost an hour with the pope on 21 December, and that encounter is also said to have had an impact on the document.

Through the second half of the summer, and then again in the fall after the trip to the United States, John Paul himself did a considerable amount of drafting. Writing in Polish and using simple plastic pens, he filled up sheets of unlined white paper.

Officials who saw the original said there were few corrections, the mark of a writer who knows what he wants to say before he starts composing.

A papal aide recalls a hot August afternoon when the conference "The Christian Roots of Europe" was being held at the papal summer residence in Castel Gandolfo, just south of Rome. Usually a busy pope can get away with a quick appearance and a brief speech at such an affair, but John Paul had used the conference to spend an uninterrupted afternoon working on the encyclical.

By late November, a complete draft was in circulation, but suggestions were still being made and debated, with some changes accepted and others not. Soon after, with the text still in a substantially fluid state, a second stage of the drafting process began, with the Secretariat of State taking over responsibility for the project. Exercising strong influences over the other Curial departments, the Secretariat is a powerful bureaucratic organ that had its origins in providing papal scribes, and oversight of papal documents is one of its important prerogatives.

But, when *Sollicitudo Rei Socialis* arrived at the Secretariat, a key player had left the scene. Archbishop Giovanni Battista Re had served as chief administrator of the secretariat for many years but had just been transferred to the Congregation for Bishops. A veteran, wise in the ways of the Curia, Monsignor Re has been variously described as "the Vatican's computer" and "the best editor in Rome." His long experience in coordinating big writing projects was missed by some who worked on this encyclical.

"The text is covered with appendages that are stuck on to the main body with some pretty thin glue," said one of the many Vatican officials who complained that the encyclical seems to be going in too many directions at once.

Passages dealing with the nonaligned movement, terrorism, and international debt were added in later stages of drafting. So was a section that calls for reforms in the world trade and monetary systems, in the terms of technology transfer, and in the structures of international organizations; but the section deals with these big projects in only the most general terms. Another insert involved a recommendation that the Church sell its precious objects to raise funds for the poor. Vatican officials have laboriously insisted that this is a symbolic suggestion, but the text remains both straightforward and enigmatic.

No foreign travels appeared on the pope's schedule between his visit to the United States in September 1987 and the May 1988 Latin American tour. Suspicious reporters noted that the pope had not sat still that long since he was recovering from the May 1981 assassination attempt. During this long spell, Dr. Navarro, the spokesman, even came up with a standard response: "The Pope is on a trip to the Curia."

Other projects, such as a long-delayed restructuring of the Curia and a consistory to name many new cardinals, help explain this lull. Yet the writing of the encyclical was also one of the major reasons for the pope's many visits to an institution that resembles other executive bureaucracies in one key respect: its own personality and biases endure, while its successive elected leaders remain transients.

Over the last decade, John Paul has worked hard to internationalize the personnel of the Curia by appointing men from many nations to jobs held for centuries by Italians. The writing of the encyclicals appears to have been another instrument in John Paul's long effort to broaden the Curia's outlook. "For this pope, the Catholic point of view must be weighted towards the third world and especially Latin America because that is where most Catholics live, and the encyclical was written from that perspective," said a Vatican official.

This is clearest in the encyclical's acerbic condemnation of the East-West rivalry. Both capitalism and communism come in for equal doses of harsh criticism as imperfect systems. The division of humanity into two hostile camps in which each exercises its own form of imperialism is said to subject the world to "structures of sin." However, the encyclical urges the Third World to adopt values like democracy and free enterprise which are more cherished in the West than the East.

The harsh concept of the superpower clash as a major cause of injustice in North-South relations was articulated even in the original schema. But it developed and expanded during the writing of the encyclical in a way that illustrates the many influences that helped shape the document.

The charge that the superpowers practice imperialism and neocolonialism to the detriment of developing nations was not made merely on the basis of abstractions. The Vatican's foreign affairs experts were asked to examine the issue, and they produced a report focusing on Africa and especially Angola. That nation is rich in natural resources, but its people are worse off than when they gained independence, largely because of a civil war that pits a regime supported by Soviet advisors and Cuban troops against insurgents backed by South Africa and the West. On 9 September 1987, when the encyclical was advancing out of its formative stage, the pope received in audience Angola's president, Jose Eduardo Dos Santos, who has been trying to negotiate concessions from South Africa so that the Cubans will leave his country and the war will end.

Several officials familiar with the drafting of the encyclical said its view of the superpowers evolved from the idea that neither East nor West provides poor nations with a model for real moral and material development. John Paul has frequently condemned Marxism as a system fundamentally in error in a variety of ways. Thus, even inside the Vatican, many were surprised to see that the encyclical repeatedly treats capitalism on an equal footing.

Here the example of Latin America played an important role. Part of the intellectual process that produced the encyclical was an examination of how the world had changed for better or worse in the two decades since Paul VI wrote *Populorum Progressio*, which this document celebrates. According to several officials, one of the conclusions was that the United States had failed to promote economic and political development in Latin America. Another, they added, was that on a higher plane the United States could no longer be said to offer a model to be emulated within the Western Hemisphere because of its own economic and moral failings.

That thought was stated rather explicitly by the most influential man in the pope's inner circle, Cardinal Ratzinger, who said in a 1985 speech that "despite all the adjustments the market system has undergone, we can no longer view the liberal capitalistic systems as the salvation of the world without reservations, as was still possible in the Kennedy era with its Peace Corps optimism."

Cardinal Ratzinger also attacked the West, and the United States specifically, for its moral decline, philosophic frivolity, and pernicious materialism. He has expressed concern that these evils are being aggressively exported to the Third World and to Latin America especially.

"It is a paradox—albeit not too much of one—that faith seems to be more secure in the East, where it is officially prosecuted," said Cardinal Ratzinger in 1985.

The encyclical follows an ancient formula by ending with the following sentence above the pope's signature: "Given in Rome, at Saint Peter's, on 30 December of the year 1987, the tenth year of my Pontificate."

In fact, on that date, a deadline set by protocol, there was no final text for the pope to sign. In the frescoed offices of the Vatican's Apostolic Palace, men wearing signs of authority like crimson sashes and silver crosses still could not agree on exactly what the encyclical would say. And the man dressed in white was repeatedly reworking the text to ensure it met his intentions.

Vatican protocol required that it be dated within the year of the anniversary it celebrates, but the actual date on which John Paul signed the final text is not a matter of public history at this point. One episode raises the question, though.

The signing of an encyclical does not involve any great ceremony, but it is still an official event to be recorded by the official photographer so that a picture can be published in the official newspaper, L'Observatore Romano, along with the text of the document, in Latin of course.

A strikingly informal photograph was published by the papacy's journal of record on 20 February, the day after Sollicitudo Rei Socialis was publicly presented. Pen in hand, John Paul sits at the desk in his private study. Other work seems to have been just set aside. Only the number two man at the Secretariat of State, Archbishop Eduardo Martinez Somalo, is in attendance, during what seems to be just another moment during an ordinary day.

The picture is also striking because it is so similar to the one published eleven months earlier along with John Paul's previous encyclical, Redemptoris Mater. In fact, it takes only a second glance to recognize that they are two photographs of the same event, the signing of the earlier encyclical.

Much remains to be learned about the writing—and the intellectual arguments—that went into this encyclical.